The Eiffel Tower

Other titles in the *History's Great Structures* series include:

C.1

History's Great
STRUCTURES

The Eiffel Tower

Adam Woog

ReferencePoint
Press®

San Diego, CA

© 2014 ReferencePoint Press, Inc.
Printed in the United States

For more information, contact:
ReferencePoint Press, Inc.
PO Box 27779
San Diego, CA 92198
www. ReferencePointPress.com

LIBRARY OF CONGRESS CATALOGING-IN-PUBLICATION DATA

Woog, Adam, 1953-
  The Eiffel Tower / by Adam Woog.
     pages cm. -- (History's great structures)
  Includes bibliographical references and index.
  ISBN-13: 978-1-60152-532-1 (hardback)
  ISBN-10: 1-60152-532-X (hardback)
  1. Tour Eiffel (Paris, France)--Juvenile literature. [1. Eiffel Tower (Paris, France)] I. Title.
  NA2930.W66 2013
  725'.970944361--dc23
                                                                 2012042907

CONTENTS

Important Events in the History of the Eiffel Tower   6

Introduction   8
  The Iron Lady

Chapter One   13
  The Background

Chapter Two   26
  The Design

Chapter Three   39
  The Construction

Chapter Four   52
  Public Reaction

Chapter Five   66
  The Eiffel Tower Today

Source Notes   83

Facts About the Eiffel Tower   86

For Further Research   88

Index   90

Picture Credits   95

About the Author   96

IMPORTANT EVENTS IN THE HISTORY OF THE EIFFEL TOWER

1884
Two of Eiffel's employees, Maurice Koechlin and Émile Nougier, begin to develop the idea of a massive iron tower, originally to propose for the 1888 world's fair in Barcelona, Spain.

1880
Eiffel begins work on one of his most important projects, designing and building the framework for the Statue of Liberty.

1887
Ground is broken for construction of the Eiffel Tower.

1879
Eiffel buys out his partner and renames the firm Compagnie des établissements Eiffel.

1888
The basic structure up to the second platform is finished.

1860   1870   1880   1890

1832
Alexandre-Gustave Eiffel is born in Dijon, France.

1886
A more fully developed and elegant version of Koechlin and Nougier's Barcelona design wins the Paris competition.

1868
Eiffel and a partner form the engineering firm Eiffel et Cie, which specializes in large iron structures.

1889
The tower is officially completed on March 31 and opens to the public on May 6.

1930
The tower loses the title of world's tallest structure when the Chrysler Building is completed in New York City.

2012
A major restoration project, focusing primarily on the first level of the tower, begins.

2002
The tower receives its 200 millionth guest.

1910 **1940** **1970** **2000**

1909
The original contract stating that the tower would be dismantled this year is overruled.

1980
A five-year restoration of the tower begins.

1898
Eiffel sends the first successful radio transmission from the tower.

1957
The first permanent radio antenna is added to the top of the tower.

1940
German soldiers occupying Paris during World War II climb to the top of the tower and briefly raise a Nazi flag.

The Iron Lady

For many people the Eiffel Tower is the first image that comes to mind when they think of Paris, France. It dominates the city's skyline, it draws visitors from around the world, and it is instantly recognizable to people near and far. The Eiffel Tower is an enduring symbol of France. The distinguished architect Le Corbusier has characterized the tower this way: "In every heart, the sign of beloved Paris, the beloved sign of Paris."[1]

The masterpiece of Alexandre-Gustave Eiffel (known to most people as Gustave) was meant to be a temporary feature of the Paris environs. The Iron Lady, as it became known, was to remain standing for only twenty years, after which the massive iron structure would be dismantled and sold for scrap. Fortunately for the world, that plan did not come to pass.

Science, Technology, and Patriotism

The Eiffel Tower was built to serve as the grand centerpiece of the Exposition Universelle, a world's fair held in Paris in 1889. It was intended as a symbol of the fair's main themes: the celebration of France's cultural achievements and the dramatic advances in science and technology then taking place. But it had another ambitious purpose: boosting French patriotism and pride that was suffering after years of political upheaval. So in large part the exposition was a way to bring the people of France together, forgetting their differences in a celebration that would assert their country's place as a leader in manufacturing, culture, and science.

Eiffel fervently believed that his tower would be an artistic triumph as well. Writer Jill Jonnes comments, "American and British engineers had likewise dreamed of building a wonderfully tall tower, but they had not been able to figure out the means to do so. Eiffel, the Frenchman, . . . had solved the mystery, and being thoroughly Gallic [French], he intended to build with elegance and artistry."[2]

A Bold Idea

When Eiffel's proposal was put before the fair's organizers, nothing even remotely like it had ever been built. At 1,023.6 feet (312 m), it would be nearly twice as high as the tallest structure in the world at the time—the Washington Monument, which was 555 feet (169 m) tall. After it was built, the Eiffel Tower continued to hold that record for more than forty years—until 1930, when the Chrysler Building in New York City surpassed it by a fraction at 1,046 feet (319 m). Radio and television antennas atop the Eiffel Tower have since brought its full height to its current 1,069 feet (325 m).

The man behind this daring proposal was already one of France's preeminent engineers when he submitted his plan to the organizers of the world's fair. His reputation had been built on designing and building large iron structures, notably bridges, in innovative and economical ways. Even though the tower would bear his name, Eiffel had little to do with the details of its design. That task fell to three senior members of his company, who did the actual design work and the calculations that would make the tower's construction possible.

Nonetheless, Eiffel was always the linchpin of the project. He oversaw the initial designs for the giant structure. His flair for presentation and marketing his projects ensured that he won the competition to build the fair's signature structure. He worked tirelessly to convince the public that his tower would be awe inspiring. And he directed its construction with precision and skill. In short, Eiffel was a brilliant businessman and entrepreneur, and it is fitting that the tower bears his name. Museum curator and writer Henri Loyrette comments, "Although it is true that Gustave Eiffel had

WORDS IN CONTEXT

entrepreneur
A person who creates independent businesses, often taking on the financial risks by him- or herself.

9

The Eiffel Tower, a symbol of French cultural and technological achievements in the late 1800s, held center stage at the Exposition Universelle, the 1889 Paris world's fair. The tower was originally intended as a temporary structure, to be dismantled after twenty years.

no hand in the design of the . . . tower, only he could have carried out such a venture."[3]

He and his colleagues had the help of hundreds of people—engineers, draftsmen, ironworkers, and other laborers—who, after years of painstaking work, together made his dream come true. The result of this combination of artistic vision and practical work is a structure that, from today's perspective, seems impossible to imagine as existing in any other form. That is, it seems to many to be complete on its own, needing nothing else to make it better. Writer Bill Bryson comments, "In its finished state, the Eiffel Tower seems so singular and whole, so couldn't-be-otherwise, that we have to remind ourselves that it is an immensely complex assemblage, a fretwork of eighteen thousand intricately fitted parts, which come together only because of an immense amount of the very cleverest thought."[4]

Public Reaction

The tower design sparked controversy before, during, and after its construction. Its supporters marveled at its extraordinary shape and height. Édouard Lockroy, the fair's commissioner, called it "A monument unique in the world [and] one of the most interesting curiosities of the capital."[5] Others were much less enthusiastic. Many people saw it as a flagrant waste of money and an ugly eyesore. Eiffel always brushed aside such criticisms, insisting that the tower would be both practical and beautiful.

In the decades since the Eiffel Tower's completion, many buildings have surpassed it in terms of height. Some of them, such as New York City's Empire State Building, are just as famous and just as cherished. The current record holder, the Burj Khalifa in the United Arab Emirates, dwarfs the Eiffel Tower, soaring an astonishing 2,716 feet (828 m) in the air. Still, few of these buildings

Famous Buildings: A Comparison of Heights

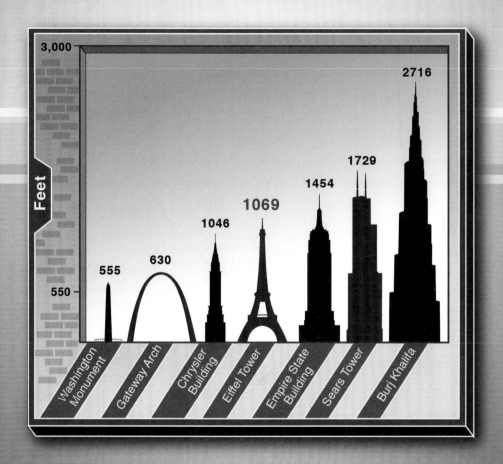

are as charismatic as Eiffel's masterpiece. Jonnes writes, "Mega-skyscrapers long ago overshadowed the Eiffel Tower's status as the world's tallest structure. Yet no man-made artifact has ever rivaled the tower's potent mixture of spare elegance, amazing enormity and complexity when experienced firsthand."[6] In short, even after more than a century the Eiffel Tower continues to fascinate and inspire the world.

CHAPTER ONE

The Background

The roots of the 1889 Exposition Universelle in Paris can be traced to a cataclysmic event that took place exactly one hundred years earlier. This event, the French Revolution, was one of the most important episodes in the history of France. For many centuries French kings and queens had ruled with absolute authority. Supporting them was a complex system of dukes, barons, and other aristocrats—all members of the ruling class. These royal figures enjoyed great wealth and essentially complete power over the lives of common people through practices such as heavy taxation and a lack of civil rights.

WORDS IN CONTEXT

aristocrats
People who are part of the ruling or noble class.

But the French people grew increasingly resentful of aristocratic rule, and in 1789 this discontent reached the boiling point. A rebellion took shape. This uprising, the French Revolution, was marked by a decade of extreme violence—most notably against the royals and aristocrats and anyone else who opposed the new order. The most famous of these unfortunate victims were King Louis XVI and his queen, Marie Antoinette. In the wake of the monarchy and its aristocratic regime came a new form of government, the First Republic, based on the then-radical concepts of *liberté, égalité, et fraternité*—liberty, equality, and fraternity. These ideals were similar to those that fueled the American Revolution in the United States a few years earlier.

Political Tension

As 1889 approached, the French government wanted to do something special to commemorate the one hundredth anniversary of the French Revolution. Authorities also wanted a way to defuse the tense political climate that had been building in France since the 1870s. That turmoil stemmed primarily from the Franco-Prussian War of 1870–1871, which pitted France against the Kingdom of Prussia (now part of Germany). This conflict, rooted in years of animosity between the two nations, led to widespread food shortages and a brutal bombardment of Paris. The war ended in victory for Prussia and, as part of the spoils of war, the winning nation was able to form a government in France that was sympathetic to its own royal leader, Emperor Wilhelm I.

The dominance of monarchist Prussia over France naturally outraged those French citizens committed to maintaining their nation as free and democratic. A group of French radicals in the capital city formed a rebel alliance called the Paris Commune. The issue of Paris operating as an independent entity was especially important to the Communards, as these radicals were called. The Commune's armed members managed to briefly take over and occupy Paris from mid-March until late May 1871, when French soldiers loyal to the Prussian-controlled government defeated them in bloody battle.

"Reconciliation, Rehabilitation, and Imperial Supremacy"

However, the dramatic standoff between the Communards and the government did not resolve itself in the 1870s or 1880s. The tense situation was made worse by dissension among various factions on both sides, coupled with a serious economic depression. By the early 1880s the Third Republic, as the current French government was known, was in serious danger of collapse.

In 1884, as a way of easing the political tension, French prime minister Jules Ferry proposed a major world's fair. It would take place in 1889, on the anniversary of the Revolution—specifically the an-

Visitors enjoy a day at the Exposition Universelle, which had its roots in the cataclysmic events of the French Revolution one hundred years earlier. As depicted in a painting by the French impressionist Jean Béraud, the Eiffel Tower could be seen from all locations at the fair.

niversary of the storming of the notorious Bastille prison, which had been destroyed in the revolutionary uprising and, a century later, was still the most potent symbol of rebellion.

Ferry's hope was that the opposing sides could suspend their differences for the duration of the exposition, creating an atmosphere of peace and healing the rifts between factions by bringing them together in a common cause.

It was also hoped that the construction and operation of the fair would be a boost to the nation's flagging economy. Not least among its purposes, meanwhile, was to raise the morale of the French by demonstrating to the world that their nation was still a major figure in global culture, politics, and science and technology. In this way, the planned fair was in large part designed to raise the prestige of the French nation among the other nations of the world.

To this end Ferry proposed a motto that would embrace all of the goals of the exposition: Reconciliation, Rehabilitation, and Imperial Supremacy. (Ferry used the word *imperial* here in the sense of "majestic" or "grand," not "royal.") Scholar Ly Y. Bui sums up these aspects of the fair's goals by stating, "The exposition would portray the Third Republic in a prestigious light, restoring pride and confidence in the flagging government. It would boost the economy, bolster the metal industry with the erection of immense pavilions, and create new job opportunities for workers."[7]

The Fair

The French government approved the idea for a fair, which was to be called the Exposition Universelle de 1889, and together with the organizers began the enormous amount of planning that needed to be done to make it a reality. The fair would be held in several locations, but its heart was the Champ de Mars. This was an open space in the central part of Paris, covering nearly 0.4 square miles (1 sq km). The Champ de Mars stretched (as it still does) from the banks of the Seine, the large river that cuts through central Paris, to the city's famed École Militaire (Military School). This stretch of land was to be the site of a number of massive buildings housing a wide variety of exhibits.

Many of these exhibits would reflect the fair's official overall theme of science and technology, which were vitally important issues for the times. The second half of the nineteenth century was a period that built on the innovations of the Industrial Revolution, when machines and factories began to dominate the old methods of manufacturing products by hand. A new age was dawning as industry became an integral part of urban life, and science and technology were crucial to advancing this explosion of industry. Although the emphasis would naturally be on French achievements in these fields, the exposition's organizers invited many other nations to build pavilions showing off their own scientific successes and significant aspects of their own cultures.

All of the pavilions were essentially complete in time for the fair's grand opening on May 6, 1889. It was a moment that had been eagerly anticipated by the exposition's organizers as well as most of the public. In a speech at the opening ceremony French president Nicolas Sadi Carnot summarized the event's overall themes. He stated,

Today France glorifies the dawn of a great century which has opened a new era in the history of mankind. Today we contemplate, in its brilliancy and in its splendor, the work born of this century of labor and of progress. . . . Our dear France is worthy

⬡ UNITING A NATION

In addition to celebrating the anniversary of the French Revolution and a new age of science and technology, there was another reason for proposing that Paris host a world's fair in 1889: politics.

France's government at the time, known as the Third Republic, had been born after the French emperor Napoléon III was overthrown in 1870. (This Napoléon was the nephew of the more famous Napoléon Bonaparte.) The new government was deeply conservative, and its power rested in politicians who were open to the possibility of restoring an emperor. This group was fiercely opposed by a large contingent that sought to bring back the reforms and ideals of the French Revolution: democracy, freedom, and equality. Gradually this more liberal faction, the Republicans, gained power and by the early 1880s dominated French politics. They succeeded in creating a number of governmental reforms, such as the establishment of free education.

But the ideals of the Third Republic's early days remained strong among many French citizens. They remained deeply committed to conservative traditions, such as supporting France's military and maintaining its close ties to Catholicism. The conflict between this faction and the reform-minded Republicans grew so strong that by the early 1880s the entire French government seemed on the brink of breaking down. Defusing this tense situation became a major factor behind the government's proposal for a massive world's fair, in the hope that the project would unite the nation in a single, shared goal.

of attracting to her the chosen of the peoples. She has the right to be proud of herself and to celebrate with head erect the economic centenary, as also the political centenary, of 1889.[8]

A Great Success

From the outset, the fair was a great success. More than 32 million visitors from all over the world, but especially from Europe, the United States, and Asia, attended. They were treated to an array of exotic pavilions, restaurants, theaters, and exhibit halls. Some of the pavilions and exhibits were cultural or scientific in nature, while others stressed the commercial products of the participating nations. A small railway, about 2 miles (3.2 km) in length, provided transportation for visitors who did not want to stroll through the entire grounds.

Many of the exhibition halls were cultural pavilions. France created many of these exhibits, including a hall that displayed the Imperial Diamond, a priceless jewel that had been discovered in South Africa in 1884—only a few years before the fair opened. Other pavilions were sponsored by nations that were eager to educate the French public about their own traditions of dress, housing, music, dance, and other topics. Participants included Japan, Persia (now Iran), Turkey, Egypt, Russia, Greece, and many Latin American nations.

Some nations boycotted the exposition, not wanting to be associated with an event that commemorated the French Revolution. Notably, the German government chose not to participate because of continued ill feelings dating from the days of the Franco-Prussian War and its aftermath. However, the German government did allow some German manufacturers to display their products to take advantage of the commercial benefits of worldwide exposure.

These pavilions also hosted a variety of performances, including dance recitals and new music by prominent composers. The most popular event—every performance was sold out, and it was the talk of all Paris—was the Wild West Show organized by the famous American buffalo hunter, soldier, and entrepreneur Buffalo Bill Cody. This spectacular display featured demonstrations of cattle roping and mock battles between cowboys and Native Americans. The extravaganza featured two hundred horses and twenty buffalo, as well as a performance by the show's star: the legendary sharpshooter Annie Oakley.

The fair's overall theme of new technology dominated many of its attractions and displays. Prominent among these exhibits were several cutting-edge innovations from the famous American inventor Thomas Edison. One of the most impressive of these was the practical application of a startling new invention, the electric lightbulb. Electric lighting was shown off in its own exhibit, and it was also used to light up the exposition's acreage at night in a dazzling display.

Another of Edison's inventions—the phonograph—was the star exhibit in another massive display of new technology housed in the Galerie des Machines (Machinery Hall). This iron and glass structure was, at the time, the longest single-span building in the world. Its main exhibition hall was 1,270 feet (387 m) long and 460 feet (140 m) wide, which made it the largest unobstructed floor area of any building in history to that point. The hall was so big that even the largest exhibits in it, such as locomotives, seemed small. Huge "moving sidewalks" transported visitors above the exhibition hall so they could gaze down on the wonders below. Years later, a man who was thirteen years old when he visited the hall recalled, "I remember very clearly the hallucinatory [ride] above whirlpools of . . . creakings, whistles, sirens, and black caverns containing circles, pyramids, and cubes."[9]

A Most Extraordinary Idea

These displays of culture and science were impressive on their own. But one aspect of the exposition was, by far, the most dazzling of them all. This was the gargantuan Eiffel Tower, which served as the main entrance to the fairgrounds. The concept of a giant tower had been part of the central planning of the exposition since the fair's earliest stages. The event's organizers, eager to create an extraordinary symbol of the exposition's theme, had in 1884 announced an open competition for its construction, which was specified to reach a proposed height of 984 feet (300 m). The competition received more than one hundred designs, some of which were outlandish or would be clearly impossible to build. For example, one submission proposed a 900-foot model (274.3 m) of a guillotine. Another idea was for a huge lighthouse that would light up all of Paris. Still another was for a gar-

Gustave Eiffel (pictured) envisioned a work of extraordinary grace and size. He ultimately came to view his tower as an artistic triumph.

gantuan sprinkler system designed to douse fires or relieve drought in the neighborhoods surrounding the Champ de Mars.

A commission assembled by the fair's organizers was given the responsibility of examining the various proposals, and by June 1886 announced that every plan but one was either impractical, insufficiently worked out, or simply bizarre. A winner was then announced: Gustave Eiffel, who proposed a tower in the shape of a giant pylon, composed of four legs that tapered to the top, forming a kind of elongated pyramid. The first public mention of this design was in the newspaper *Le Figaro* in late October 1884, which noted that Eiffel's planned tower was shaping up to be the most extraordinary aspect of the future fair.

The Man Behind the Tower

At this time, Eiffel was France's leading structural engineer and a well-known, highly respected figure. Eiffel had been born in Dijon, in east-central France, in 1832. He had shown a knack for the basics of engineering at a young age, excelling in his understanding of mathematics, physics, and science. He also apparently inherited a flair for successfully operating a business. Perhaps he inherited some of his business sense from his mother, Catherine, who expanded the family business into a large coal-distribution operation. It proved so successful that her husband, Alexandre, gave up his job as an administrator for the French army in order to assist her.

Eiffel graduated from Dijon's Lycée Royale (the equivalent to a high school) with degrees in humanities and science. He went on to attend several colleges before graduating in 1855 from the École Centrale des Arts et Manufactures, an engineering university in Paris. Eiffel graduated from this school near the top of his class—thirteenth out of eighty students. By all accounts this high ranking was due as much to his perseverance and work ethic as to his brilliance as a student.

A "SLIGHTLY STRANGE PLEASURE"

Before the tower was built, Eiffel frequently lectured and spoke publicly about possible practical uses for it. But, as writer Bill Bryson points out, the motivation behind Eiffel's endeavor likely had little or nothing to do with practicality.

> The Eiffel Tower wasn't just the largest thing that anyone had ever proposed to build, it was the largest completely useless thing. . . . Eiffel gamely insisted that his tower would have many practical uses—that it would make a terrific military lookout and that one could do useful aeronautical and meteorological experiments from its upper reaches—but eventually even he admitted that mostly he wished to build it simply for the slightly strange pleasure of making something really quite enormous.

Bill Bryson, *At Home*. New York: Anchor, 2010, pp. 251–52.

His original plan, to join the staff of his uncle's vinegar factory in Dijon, was canceled after a family quarrel and financial troubles at the factory. Instead, young Eiffel found work as the personal secretary to a railway engineer and followed this job with a stint as an engineer for a railway company. In time he rose to the position of head of the company's research department. Bill Bryson notes that Eiffel excelled at the work: "He was, to put it mildly, very good at it. He built bridges and viaducts across impossible defiles [narrow valleys], railway concourses of stunning expansiveness, and other grand and challenging structures that continue to impress and inspire."[10]

Eiffel's experience during this period in designing and building railway bridges set him on his future path. He rose quickly through the ranks and became the company's chief engineer. Eiffel relished every aspect of the work, from the mathematics and physics needed to imagine and design a project to solving the technical problems of construction. And he liked to be present during the construction phase, regularly visiting the job sites, where he could work directly with the construction supervisors and workers.

Early Successes

Eager to make a name for himself, Eiffel decided to strike off on his own in 1868. He partnered with another engineer, Théophile Seyrig, to form the firm Eiffel et Cie (Eiffel and Company). The firm specialized in the design and construction of large-scale iron bridges and buildings. Eiffel established his office and workshop in Levallois-Perret, a suburb of Paris, and the new company quickly found success. In time the firm added offices or representatives in such far-flung locations as China, Argentina, Russia, and Italy.

Among the company's early projects was the design of key elements in the large exhibition hall for the 1878 Exposition Universelle in Paris (which preceded the 1889 fair that would make Eiffel famous). Eiffel et Cie also completed such innovative projects as building an all-metal church building, which was shipped in pieces to Arica, Chile, and assembled on-site. Other important projects for Eiffel et Cie during this period included the Maria Pia Bridge in Portugal, which was at the time the longest single-arch span in the world. This massive project demonstrated Eiffel's ability to create elegant and simple designs with relatively inexpensive materials and new construction techniques, and to complete projects within limited budgets and time frames.

Still another notable project during this time was an innovative railway terminal in the Hungarian city of Pest (now part of Budapest). Eiffel used techniques that were then highly unusual and that would later become key elements in his famous tower. Notably, he chose not to hide the building's metal framework—that is, the guts of the terminal—behind the usual decorative facade. Eiffel later noted about the project that it combined artistic elegance with practicality, since the building's decorative features were also its structural elements.

WORDS IN CONTEXT
facade
Exterior siding on a building.

But perhaps Eiffel's major accomplishment during this middle part of his career was the Garabit Viaduct, a 1,854-foot bridge (565 m) crossing a river in the mountains of the rugged Massif Central region in south-central France. In the opinion of some experts, this was an accomplishment to rival his more famous tower. Architect and writer Bertrand Lemoine comments that the Garabit Viaduct "still stands as a masterpiece in Eiffel's career."[11]

In 1879, by now solidly established as the leading engineer in the field of iron structures, Eiffel bought out his business partner and became the sole owner of his company, renaming it the Compagnie des établissements Eiffel. This new firm's accomplishments included a method for building prefabricated bridge kits, ranging in size from footbridges to railway bridges. Their most notable advantage was that these kits could easily be transported in pieces to remote locations and assembled on the spot.

Two Iconic Structures

The biggest and most famous projects that Eiffel took on during this period involved one of the world's most familiar and beloved icons: the Statue of Liberty in New York Harbor, a gift from France to the United States. This powerful symbol of freedom had (and still has) an exterior of thin but enormously heavy copper sheets. This facade needed a strong framework to support it, and the statue's designer, sculptor Frédéric Bartholdi, specifically chose Eiffel to create this interior framework. In fact, building the statue would have been impossible without Eiffel's contributions. In short, Eiffel's deep knowledge of how large metal structures could be successfully built proved to be vital to the project. Henri Loyrette remarks, "Although the Statue of Liberty seems to many to stand apart from the rest of Eiffel's work, he himself saw it differently. Despite the 'artistic' covering which completely concealed the work he had carried out, it can nevertheless be seen as a continuation of his earlier work."[12]

Eiffel's firm began work on the immensely complex Statue of Liberty project in 1880. As with Bartholdi's exterior, Eiffel's skeleton for the statue was built and partially assembled in France, then shipped to the statue's permanent home for its formal unveiling on July 4, 1884. Eiffel's role in this endeavor proved to be one of the crowning achievements in his career, although this role still remains largely unknown to the public. But he would soon begin work on an even more powerful and enduring symbol of a great nation, one that, as Bryson points out, took his ideas to an extreme and made him a household word: "In his next big project he made sure no one would fail to appreciate his role in its construction, by creating something that was nothing *but* skeleton."[13] That "something," of course, was the tower that still bears Eiffel's name.

CHAPTER TWO

The Design

After Eiffel won the competition to design and build the exposition's tower, he spent many months negotiating the details with Paris city officials. The negotiations were a lengthy and often frustrating process, in part because so many governmental organizations had to give the project their approval. The process dragged on so long that Eiffel almost abandoned the project. At one point he noted in a letter to the fair authorities, "I would be very sorry to renounce the construction of what most agree will be one of the Exposition's principal attractions."[14]

Eventually the two sides came to an agreement, and a contract was signed in January 1887. The project's budget was set at 8 million francs (roughly $58 million in today's US dollars). The Parisian government granted Eiffel 1.5 million francs toward his construction costs, which was less than a quarter of the estimated total. Eiffel offered to cover a substantial amount of the remaining cost and raise the rest from investors. In return, Parisian authorities agreed to give him the profits from admission sales for twenty years—the amount of time the tower was scheduled to remain standing. The contract further stated that Eiffel would donate 10 percent of these profits to the poor of Paris. (There is no evidence that this last stipulation was ever fulfilled.)

Design Work Begins

Once the contract was signed, the design work could begin in earnest. Some of this work had already been done. The basic form of the proposed tower had been created long before Eiffel even submitted his plans to the exposition's committee. This was because Eiffel's winning entry was not the first time his firm had proposed building a giant tower. He had submitted a similar but less elegant design to an earlier world's fair, the Exposición Universal (Universal Exposition) of 1888 in Barcelona, Spain.

But that city's authorities had rejected the idea: It was too strange, too expensive, and too much out of context with the city's overall design. Undaunted, Eiffel did not abandon the idea. Instead, he had his first design reworked and submitted it again for the fair in Paris. The idea was essentially the same: to build a structure that stressed simplicity and practicality but with added touches that made it far more elegant than the Barcelona proposal.

In many ways, both the failed Barcelona project and the Eiffel Tower were essentially refinements of work that the engineer had done often in the past. He had already perfected many aspects of the tower's design—in some ways, the new project simply turned Eiffel's previous work on its side. In other words, the tower used many of the same principles of bridge building—it simply moved the construction toward the sky instead of across a valley or river. Architectural historian Barry Bergdoll comments, "The overscaled pylon was in fact a logical extension of the research into structure and fabrication that had made possible the firm's most successful projects of the previous decade, most famously the monumental railroad viaduct at Garabit in the Massif Central."[15]

The Basic Design

Although Eiffel usually receives full credit for the tower that bears his name, in fact he was not responsible for its basic concept. Two of Eiffel's senior engineers, Maurice Koechlin and Émile Nougier, had begun work on the Barcelona proposal some five years before the Parisian tower was built. Koechlin's preliminary drawings envisioned a giant structure 984 feet (300 m) tall. In most respects the early plans he and Nougier developed were essentially the same as what was finally built. Henri Loyrette comments, "It was in fact as early as 1884 that Nouguier and Koechlin ... had come up with the idea of 'a very high tower;' on June 6 of the same year, Koechlin drew a sketch of the construction they had thought up, 'a great pylon con-sisting of four ... girders standing apart at the base and coming together at the top-joined to one another by metal trusses at regular intervals.'"[16]

The shape Koechlin proposed thus looked something like an elongated pyramid. Its four gently curving girders (the vertical legs) would be held up with truss-es (frameworks that strengthen and support the girders) placed at regular intervals. The legs would support three platforms above street level. Two of these levels were to be public viewing platforms.

The first level would be 187 feet (57 m) from the ground and roughly 45,200 square feet (4,200 sq m) in area. This left plenty of space for such amenities as a restaurant, a bar, a 250-seat theater, and a viewing promenade 8.5 feet (2.6 m) wide that would provide visitors with a spectacular view. The second level would be 377.2 feet (115 m) high and have an area of some 15,000 square feet (1,400 sq m) with room for more restaurants and viewing spots. The third level was not originally planned to be open to the public, although many years later a small observation deck was added to it, and it was available to the public. This third level was to be 905.5 feet (276 m) off the ground and would house a small apartment and workshop for Eiffel. In time, af-ter it was completed, the apartment was lavishly decorated with such elegant touches as oil paintings, a piano, and velvet-fringed couches.

Perfecting the Design

Eiffel liked many aspects of Koechlin and Nougier's concept as it was revamped for the Parisian contest. For example, he liked the idea of adding two levels that would include restaurants and other attractions. But he was not satisfied with the concept for the overall look of the tower. The original plan was stark and unadorned—little more than a dull assemblage of girders. It would have appeared a little like the sort of tower that today is used for supporting electrical cables across long distances.

Eiffel saw the design as practical, but it did not impress him as beautiful or pleasing to the eye. So Eiffel commissioned a respected

Work begins at the base of one of the tower's four legs. The design called for a structure that resembled an elongated pyramid, with four gently curving legs, or girders, held in place by supporting trusses.

Parisian architect, Stephen Sauvestre, to join the team and make improvements. Sauvestre's contributions included horizontal, curved grillwork arches, more artistically pleasing pedestals, a bulb-shaped design for the top, and various improvements to the public viewing areas and restaurants, such as a glass pavilion on the first level.

All of Sauvestre's additions were purely decorative, not structural—that is, they were not necessary to the tower's strength or safety. However, they did make the tower more beautiful, and—perhaps just as important—they also made it *appear* sturdier. This, Eiffel knew, would be a key element in reassuring the exposition's committee and, later, the public about its safety.

Iron Versus Steel

Designing the tower was only part of the process. Another important element was to settle on the type of material that Eiffel would use to build it. He considered steel but ultimately rejected it; steel was a new and relatively untested material, and Eiffel lacked confidence in how it might perform. Instead he decided to stay with what he knew best: iron. Eiffel decided on a type of iron called "puddle iron," so named because of the process used to make it. This process was in common use at the time and was well tested and reliable. It involves melting the iron into a liquid state, then swirling it to remove carbon and other impurities in the metal from the final product. The molten iron is then "puddled" into molds that help shape the iron into its final form. (Today, wrought iron, such as that used for decorative fences, is often made this way.)

Eiffel's decision to use iron instead of steel proved to be a turning point in the history of construction. Only a few years after the tower was built, the manufacture of steel was perfected. Steel soon became (and still is) the preferred material for large building construction. So the most famous structure built in the nineteenth century, one that was meant to symbolize cutting-edge technology, was made of a material that was about to be superseded by something better. Bill Bryson comments, "Never in history has a structure been more technologically advanced [but] materially obsolescent."[17]

Forgotten

Once Sauvestre had made his additions, Eiffel approved the design and instructed his employees to move forward. This involved Koechlin and Nougier taking out several design patents, which were described in the patent application as being "for a new configuration allowing the construction of metal supports and pylons capable

 THE LIMITS OF STONEWORK

Some of the proposals for a tower for the exposition were for structures that were partially or completely built of stonework, or masonry. But Eiffel knew that a structure the size and height of his tower would require a metal framework for support if masonry were used. Eiffel preferred a structure built entirely from metal, which he knew would be strong enough by itself. Henri Loyrette comments,

> Although certain that metal was to be used . . . Eiffel was still hesitating between iron and steel. At the time, he inclined towards iron, which was heavier and more resistant to buckling, and was easier to work with than steel, but he nevertheless reserved his opinion. The one thing he was certain of was that the use of masonry alone would render the project impossible. The ancient civilizations, the Middle Ages, and the Renaissance had pushed the use of stone to the limits of boldness, and [as Eiffel noted] "it hardly seems possible to go much further than our precursors using the same material."

Henri Loyrette, *Gustave Eiffel*. New York: Rizzoli, 1985, p. 114.

of exceeding a height of 300 metres."[18] However, Eiffel—who was never one to share credit—saw the financial advantage in holding the licenses that were awarded for these innovations, so he bought out Koechlin's and Nougier's shares in the patents. Eiffel promised to include the two engineers' names every time the project or the patents were mentioned, a promise that was not kept.

As a result, the two engineers and the architect have been largely forgotten in the years since. It appears that Koechlin and Nougier, at least, were not seriously resentful of this obscurity. Both remained in the company's employ for many more years. Koechlin became Eiffel et Cie's managing director when Eiffel retired, while Nougier stayed with the firm until his retirement in 1893. Sauvestre, who specialized in houses, did not formally join the company, but as an architect he went on to design many notable structures that can still be seen in Paris and elsewhere.

A Savvy Leader

These three men clearly made major contributions to the project, but they were not the ones who made it a reality. Most historians agree that credit for that achievement goes to Eiffel. His ability to take the lead on the project displayed a genius for organization and a knack for finding the people best suited to bringing the idea to life. Bertrand Lemoine comments, "Ambitious, energetic, and decisive, he possessed all the skills of a fully-trained engineer combined with originality, a realistic approach to deadlines, and an understanding of public relations, and the capacity to attract and retain the best collaborators."[19]

In his role as leader on the project Eiffel also displayed a penchant for taking the credit—after all, the tower carries his name, while the others are largely unknown to the public. Eiffel understood the importance of publicity. He had displayed a version of his company's tower design long before the Paris competition, and after his design was chosen for the exposition, Eiffel continued to lecture about it, introducing the details of the project to the public and to engineering and governmental organizations. In these lectures Eiffel outlined the formidable technical challenges that the project faced, as well as the tower's role as a symbol of the emerging industrial and technological age. Typical of his comments was the statement that his creation would stand for "not only the art of the modern engineer, but also the century of Industry and Science in which we are living and for which the way was prepared by the great scientific movements of the end of the eighteenth century and by the Revolution of 1789, to which this monument will be built as an expression of France's gratitude."[20]

Technical Challenges

Eiffel's comments about the technical challenges reflect his realistic view of the project. Nothing like this tower had ever been built before on such a grand scale, and the project's countless problems required equally countless innovative solutions. Some were small, some huge—and, of course, all of them had to be resolved many decades before computers could help calculate and catalog the vast amount of data that was required to solve problems and store information.

One prominent example of the problems Eiffel faced was the absolute necessity of maintaining accuracy where each separate piece of the tower met. The design and manufacture of each of these parts had to be precise. For example, a tiny mistake in calculation could have thrown off the angle of a leg's incline as it was built. Even a small deviation in this angle would have affected the stability of the tower, forcing Eiffel to pull the entire structure down before rebuilding. Every pair of rivet holes had to be designed to match up with such precise accuracy that they would not be more than 0.04 inches (1 mm) apart when it was time for them to be joined together.

Wind and Weather

Severe weather conditions, always a concern on large construction projects, presented additional challenges for Eiffel's team because of the tower's great height. Eiffel had years of experience in building and bridge construction, so he understood how strong winds could damage a badly designed structure. In his autobiography, written later in his life, Eiffel writes, "During the course of my career as an engineer and on account of the exceptional scale of the construction work that filled it, wind was always an absorbing subject for me. It was an enemy against which I had to anticipate a constant battle, either during the building or afterwards."[21]

The plan for the tower had Eiffel's complete confidence. He felt certain it would fulfill his goals of beauty and sturdiness. In an interview in the Parisian newspaper *Le Temps* in 1887, Eiffel states, "Now to what phenomenon did I give primary concern in designing the Tower? It was wind resistance. Well then! I hold that the curvature of the monument's four outer edges, which is as mathematical calculation dictated it should be . . . will give a great impression of strength and beauty, for it will reveal to the eyes of the observer the boldness of the design as a whole."[22]

To avoid wind damage, Eiffel and his engineers had designed the tower as a latticed, open-air structure with minimal obstacles, so that even the strongest gusts could pass right through it. Their calculations of wind resistance were so accurate that the tower swayed (and still sways) only a negligible amount in even the strongest wind. Architecture professor Annette Fierro writes, "Eiffel's calculations eventually proved highly accurate; during either strong winds or high temperatures, the top of the tower deflects [moves] less than ten centimeters."[23]

Wind was not the only climatic challenge. Eiffel's design also had to take into account heat and cold. Once again Eiffel's construction experience had prepared him for the challenge. For example, Eiffel knew that on hot days the iron tower would slightly expand and cold temperatures would cause the tower to slightly contract. Knowing this, Eiffel's team designed the tower to withstand even the most extreme weather. The team calculated the amount of expansion so precisely that even in the hottest weather the tip of the tower moves no more than about 6 inches (15 cm).

A related challenge concerned protecting the tower's exposed iron from rain and snow. Unlike steel, which was yet to be perfected as a material for construction, iron rusts unless treated with a strong coat of paint. This required a system of scaffolding that would allow workers to reach all of the tower's exposed areas—which in this case meant the entire structure—for repainting jobs. The process of repainting the tower, which has to be done approximately every seven years, is

To prevent wind damage to their tall tower, Eiffel and his engineers settled on a latticed, open-air design that would allow gusts to pass right through the structure. Their vision can clearly be seen in this close-up view of the intricate mass of ironwork during one phase of construction.

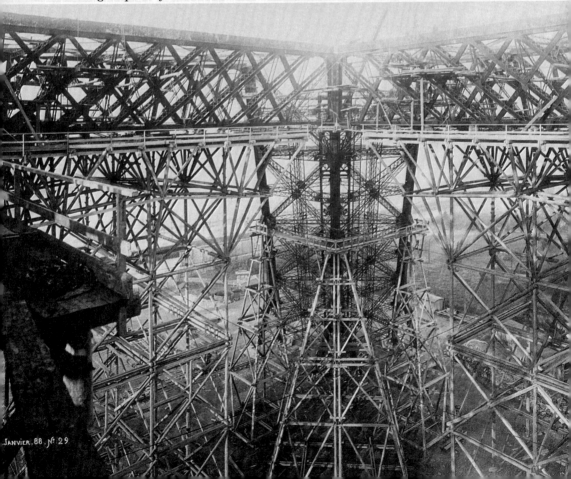

LESSONS FROM A GIANT CHOCOLATE EASTER BUNNY

The most famous structure Eiffel worked on before he built his tower was the Statue of Liberty in New York Harbor. His interior structural design cleverly allowed the statue's very thin copper skin to withstand a variety of stresses. Writer Bill Bryson notes,

> Without ingenious interior engineering to hold it up, the Statue of Liberty is merely a hollow structure of beaten copper barely one-tenth of an inch thick. That's about the thickness of a chocolate Easter bunny—an Easter bunny 151 feet high, which must stand up to wind, snow, driving rain, and salt spray; the expansion and contraction of metal in sun and cold; and a thousand other rude, daily physical assaults. None of these challenges had ever been faced by an engineer before, and Eiffel solved them in the neatest possible way, by creating a skeleton of trusses and springs on which the copper skin is worn like a suit of clothes.

Bill Bryson, *At Home*. New York: Anchor, 2010, pp. 251–52.

dangerous but necessary. Eiffel notes, "We will most likely never realize the full importance of painting the Tower, that it is the essential element in the conservation of metal works and the more meticulous the paint job, the longer the Tower shall endure."[24]

Designing the Elevators

Still another design challenge concerned the elevators. Eiffel felt that a standard elevator traveling up and down through the structure's center would ruin the simple, open look of the tower. Instead, he insisted that the elevators be designed so that they could ascend and descend along the gentle curves of the tower's legs. Jill Jonnes notes, "Eiffel, an artist in the use of iron, had refused to take the easy route of simply having an elevator rise straight up through the center of what he rightly viewed as his magnum opus, marring the uncluttered simplicity of the tower's elegant profile."[25]

Once the elevator location was decided, the challenge was to design elevators that could accommodate the expected crowds. Along with the one spiral staircase, the elevators needed to accommodate a large number of visitors—from two thousand to twenty-five hundred people every hour. Some writers and architectural historians suggest that perfecting the elevators was the single most difficult challenge in designing and building the structure. This was because, at the time, no elevator was capable of moving safely up and down a structure as high as the Eiffel Tower. So a single elevator could take visitors from the ground level, where they entered the structure, to the first level, which included a promenade, public viewing areas, a theater, and restaurants. But that same elevator did not have enough power to reach the second level, which offered additional public viewing areas and restaurants. The solution came from Léon Edoux, a prominent French inventor (and one of Eiffel's former classmates in engineering school). Edoux devised an ingenious plan.

Edoux's design involved two connected elevators in each of the tower's four legs. In each leg one elevator rose from the ground to the first level, and another elevator took visitors from the first level to the second level. Each elevator car in a set weighed some 10 tons (9 metric tons) and could carry up to sixty-five passengers at a time. The cars would not have separate counterbalances to raise and lower them, as was usual for elevators at the time. Instead, Edoux's elevators were joined together by ropes so they counterbalanced each other. When in use, elevator A would be on the ground and elevator B at the second observation level. A powerful ram pushed elevator A from the ground to the first level. Since the cars were joined, elevator B dropped from the second level to the first. When they met at the middle (the first level), passengers moved from one to the other. Then elevator A went back down, pulling elevator B back up to the second level.

This arrangement was clever, but somewhat inconvenient for passengers. They could not go all the way up in one car. Instead, they would have to walk from one elevator to the other at the first floor along a narrow gangway. This gangway offered a virtually unobstructed view of Paris, but even with sturdy safety rails the experience was not for the fainthearted.

Thousands of Drawings, Countless Calculations

All of this preparatory work required staggering amounts of handmade drawings and calculations. Forty or so designers and "calculators" (the people who did the necessary math) were assigned to the project. In fact, more time was needed to design the tower—roughly two years—than it took to build it. During this period of intense work, Eiffel's design office created some 1,700 general drawings for the skeleton alone, not counting the public viewing platforms and other areas, plus 3,629 more detailed drawings. These drawings, which required countless meticulous mathematical calculations, itemized each of the more than 18,038 different parts the tower needed.

Once this painstaking design process was complete, Eiffel and his colleagues embarked on the next stage: making their bold design a reality.

CHAPTER THREE

The Construction

The forging of the iron pieces that would form virtually every part of the tower took place at Eiffel's factory in the Parisian suburb of Levallois-Perret. As was generally true for the project as a whole, the construction of the tower moved at a swift but organized pace. Eiffel's knack for detail and preparation made the short time frame of the construction—just over two years—manageable.

For the 150 or so employees in the Levallois-Perret factory, the bulk of the work consisted of precisely casting each of the thousands of iron pieces and drilling the holes for the rivets that would hold them together. Most of these individual pieces of iron were then bolted together at the factory into segments of various sizes that could be transported more easily for final assembly at the building site. Each of these individual sections was held together with temporary bolts that were strong enough to keep them together for the journey to the Champ de Mars, but the bolts were by no means strong enough for use in the permanent structure. More permanent rivets would replace them during the building process.

The process Eiffel devised for this portion of the project served a purpose besides just efficiency. It also guaranteed that the tower would be easy to take down, and thus reassured those Parisians who were already beginning to object to the gigantic structure. Annette Fierro writes, "This system not only accommodated a compressed construction schedule, . . . it was also ideal for the likely prospect of its dismantling."[26]

At the Site

As each of the sections was completed at Eiffel's factory, horse-drawn wooden wagons carried them from there to the Champ de Mars site, a distance of some 3 miles (4.8 km). A formal groundbreaking ceremony was held on January 23, 1887, and the preliminary work began. This involved digging out tons of dirt to sink the four gigantic concrete and stone foundations that would support the tower's legs.

Each of the foundations was sunk to a depth of about 53 feet (16.2 m). These foundations rested on top of thick beds of gravel. Unlike compacted dirt, the gravel beds were slightly flexible, which would allow the tower's legs to be adjusted slightly and to later withstand tiny changes as they heated and cooled with the weather.

The work of sinking and stabilizing the east and south foundations was relatively straightforward. The job required digging a trench, building wooden walls to keep it from collapsing, laying the gravel, and pouring the concrete. However, the west and north segments required much more complex engineering and construction than the first two. The extra care in the west and north corners was necessary because these legs were situated closer to the Seine River, where the ground was less solid.

Specifically, additional support was needed to secure the two foundations that were closest to the river. They required extra reinforcements driven deep into the riverbed to keep their foundation slabs from sliding or sinking in the softer ground. Then, once these reinforcements were built and all four of the tower's concrete foundations were complete, Eiffel's workers moved on to the next phase. They installed limestone blocks on top of each of the foundations. The top surfaces of these limestone blocks were shaped so that they formed "shoes" into which the "feet" of the tower's legs would later fit, held in place by gigantic bolts.

The Tower Rises

By late June 1887, about five months into the project's on-site phase, the foundation work was complete. Now work on the tower itself

Workers prepare to lay gravel and pour concrete into deep trenches that are held open by wooden walls. Once completed, the structures will form the foundations for the tower's legs.

could begin. All of the sections from the factory were on-site and ready to go, as were a surprisingly small number of workers, considering the scale of the project and its tight deadline. Only 150 to 300 laborers were on-site at any given moment, all wearing the traditional blue work clothes and heavy wooden clogs of French construction workers.

For these laborers, assembling the huge iron pieces was like putting together a gargantuan, three-dimensional jigsaw puzzle. Each section had already been carefully marked, catalogued, and tracked so

COVERING COSTS

The contract that Eiffel signed with the organizers of the exposition included lengthy sections guaranteeing that aspects of the construction would not interfere unnecessarily with the surrounding area. For example, the contract stipulated that Eiffel was responsible for the costs of moving trees, bushes, or other plantings to make way for the tower, and that only gardeners employed by the city could do the work. Eiffel also promised to arrange for repairs, at his expense, if any surrounding buildings were damaged during construction. And city authorities also stipulated that the project would not disrupt the hydrants, sewer drains, water pipes, and other elements in the city's water supply system.

that it could be identified and properly placed. The factory measurements and other work had been so precise that the ironworkers did not need to drill new holes or reshape pieces on site. If, on occasion, they encountered a misshapen piece, it was sent back to the factory and replaced or reconfigured.

The site at the Champ de Mars was always one of intense, hard work—but work that was done efficiently and in a logical way. A visitor there commented, "250 workmen came and went in a perfectly orderly way, carrying long beams on their shoulders, climbing up and down through the lattice ironwork with surprising agility. The rapid hammer blows of the riveters could be heard, and they worked with fire that burned with the clear trembling flame of the will-o'-the-wisp."[27]

As the legs of the tower began to rise, the height and angle of each was adjusted slightly. Because of the huge size of the legs, a great deal of power was needed to make even the tiniest of these adjustments. Eiffel's crew used machines that resembled giant jackhammers to provide this power. Meanwhile, sand-filled weights kept the legs in place while they were being shifted and adjusted. Henri Loyrette comments, "This perfect organization, which won Eiffel universal praise, gave all observers the impression that the tower was constructing itself. . . . It was a smooth, well-oiled operation where human participation seemed limited, almost nonexistent."[28]

Creepers and Scaffolds

To build the lower part of the tower, the workers stood on the girders that formed the legs; they hauled up tools and building materials with the help of cranes. But the cranes could only go as high as the first level; cranes that could go higher did not yet exist. So Eiffel and his team invented steam-powered cranes they called creepers that ran along tracks on the insides of each tower leg. (These tracks would later be used for guiding the passenger elevators.)

Related to this problem was the need for scaffolds around the legs. These scaffolds were needed to support workers, equipment, and tools at increasing heights as the tower grew. Scaffolds were also needed to support the weight of the legs themselves. At this point in the construction, the legs leaned inward at a steep angle of 54 degrees and were being kept from falling over only by the huge bolts that had been sunk into the foundation. Building the tower higher without further support would have led to collapse and disaster. (In the next phase of the building process, to the second level, the angle of the legs increased even more: to a very steep 80 degrees.)

So Eiffel arranged for gigantic, progressively higher wooden scaffolds to be built around the legs. These scaffolds were strong enough to support the legs during construction, in addition to supporting all of the necessary equipment and workers. Reaching just the first level of the tower required sixteen of these scaffolds: twelve smaller ones, each about 90.5 feet (30 m) high, and four larger ones, each about 131 feet (40 m) high.

"A Colossal Spider's Web"

Much of the construction relied on the skilled ironworkers who attached each piece to its "mates." After a girder section had been brought up, the workers removed the temporary bolts that had been holding the pieces together, put the pieces into place, and replaced the temporary bolts with permanent iron rivets (about 2.5 million of them in all). The laborers then pounded each girder into position, using hydraulic jacks that could exert some 881.8 tons (800 metric tons) of force.

Twenty teams of four men each performed this grueling work. One heated the rivet over a portable furnace. The heat made it malleable and ready to be hammered into the exact shape needed. Another held the rivet in place as it was slotted into its spot. A third shaped the ends of the rivet into their correct forms while they were still hot. And a fourth beat the rivet with a sledgehammer, pounding it permanently into place. Each rivet was deliberately made a little too long, so that as it cooled from its super-heated condition its length contracted slightly and assured a tight fit.

Not surprisingly, huge crowds of Parisians and others watched the construction work with fascination, marveling as it grew higher and higher. In the spring of 1888 a reporter for the British *Evening Telegraph* newspaper wrote, "M. Eiffel's Tower of Babel is rising steadily, and the enormous mass of iron which the constructors have already piled up against the clouds is the amazement of everybody. When you stand at the base of the gigantic monument and look up into the skies through a colossal spider's web of red metal the whole thing strikes you as being one of the most daring attempts since Biblical days."[29]

Labor Issues

The riveting work and other jobs were difficult and dangerous and required long hours of heavy labor. A typical workday lasted 12 hours in

3. 7 janvier 1888.

4. 27 avril 1888.

5. 19 juin 1888.

6. 19 juillet 1888.

The Eiffel Tower gradually rises to its final height in this series of photographs taken at various stages of construction between 1888 and 1889. Crowds often gathered at the construction site to witness the tower's steady ascent.

summer, 10 to 11 hours in autumn and spring, and 9 hours in winter. Toward the end of the construction period, as the deadline drew near, workers were putting in 13-hour days.

In addition to putting up with these long days, workers frequently had to endure strong winds, freezing cold, or summertime heat. When the project had started in January 1887 Parisians were ice-skating on lakes in the city's parks. The summertime was especially hot during the construction period, with numerous threatening thunderstorms.

Eiffel paid his employees well for this hard work. But sometime in the winter of 1888 or spring of 1889 a large group of skilled workers demanded higher wages and threatened to strike if Eiffel did not agree to their demands. A strike would have seriously affected an already tight schedule. So Eiffel agreed to their demands, and the threatened walkout never occured.

Eiffel also took care of his employees in other ways. For example, once the first level was complete, he built a canteen there to feed the workers. Meals were not free, but they cost about half of what nearby cafés charged. This solved several issues at once. The laborers did not need to worry about bringing their own meals and would not need to leave the worksite. It also lessened the chance of a slip because workers did not need to scale the building down and up again just for a meal. Furthermore, it was simply more efficient: No time was wasted getting to ground level and back. (This being France, the workers had to have wine with their meals. However, Eiffel insisted that they drink only a small amount before returning to work.)

Eiffel could be both generous and stern. After he reached an agreement with the leaders of the threatened strike he fired anyone who was not present by midday of the next day. Once work resumed he humiliated the strike leaders by assigning them jobs only on the lower levels instead of more prestigious work on the higher levels.

WORKING UNDERWATER

Because two of the tower's legs were close to the Seine River, some of the work on the foundation had to be done underwater. This work was done using caissons. Caissons are specialized chambers used to create structures, such as supports for bridges, that need to be built underwater. A caisson is essentially a huge concrete compartment. It is designed so that as it descends into the water it fills with water and sinks instead of floating. When the caisson has sunk completely, the water inside the chamber is pumped out, and compressed air is pumped in. This pressurizes the chamber and allows workers to descend into it. The workers climb in and out of the caisson through sets of airlocks in the ceiling, which is kept above water. Caissons are still commonly used in underwater construction projects.

Safety

As with any large-scale construction project, many hazards existed at the tower site. The risk of falling from the tower's great height was ever present; a single slip of the foot could be disastrous. In one sense Eiffel's attitude toward this danger was simply logical. He pointed out, half seriously, that workers high on the tower should not be paid more than others—there was really no greater danger from working at higher levels, he said, since a fall of 40 feet (12 m) could kill a man as easily as a fall of 400 (122 m).

On a more serious note, Eiffel was always extremely concerned with the safety of his workers. The many precautions he took included building guardrails and screens to stop falls. These safety measures were so thorough that only two men died during the project—and one was not on the job at the time. Hoping to impress his girlfriend, he had climbed onto the partially completed structure but lost his footing and fell to his death. Another worker later died of gangrene from a wound he suffered while on-site. Eiffel made sure that the families of these men were well compensated for their losses.

"Reaping Lightning Bolts in the Clouds"

The construction work continued to move quickly; except for a few details, by the end of March 1888 the tower was finished up to the first level. Less than three months later, in June 1888, the basic structure as far as the second level was complete. The tower was now 420 feet (128 m) above the ground and already closing in on what was then the world's highest structure: the 555-foot Washington Monument (169 m).

The following month, on July 14, 1888, France celebrated Bastille Day, the nation's biggest holiday. Parisian authorities used the tower's second level as a stage for a massive fireworks display. The evening of July 14 saw a burst of exploding lights of many brilliant hues and shapes surrounding and above the rising tower.

After this grand celebration, the next weeks were spent putting the finishing touches on the second level, and it was complete by mid-August 1888. At this point, as had been true all through the project, the construction site remained one of hectic but highly organized labor. At the beginning of 1889 journalist Émile Goudeau described a visit:

> A thick cloud of tar and coal smoke seized the throat, and we were deafened by the din of metal screaming beneath the hammer. Over there they were still working on the bolts: workmen with their iron bludgeons, perched on a ledge just a few centimetres wide, took turns at striking the [rivets]. One could have taken them for blacksmiths contentedly beating out a rhythm on an anvil in some village forge, except that these smiths were not striking up and down vertically, but horizontally, and as with each blow came a shower of sparks, these black figures, appearing larger than life against the background of the open sky, looked as if they were reaping lightning bolts in the clouds.[30]

Nearly Finished

As the deadline drew near, the construction workers stepped up their pace. March 31, 1889, marked the completion of the main structure. However, the finishing touches required a great deal more work.

One of the most important of these final tasks involved the elevators. Because nothing like them had been built before, getting the elevators in working order proved to be a major challenge. Two companies had been hired to build them. A French firm, Roux, Combaluzier and Lepape, had the contract for the east and west elevators, and an American company, Otis Elevator, was responsible for the elevators on the north and south legs. Teams from both firms worked feverishly to find solutions to nagging problems that prevented the elevators from working properly.

The French newspaper *Le Figaro* had planned to publish special editions from an office and printing press in the tower. Unable to reach the second floor by elevator, the paper's staff had to make the exhausting climb up the narrow spiral stairs every day. One of the newspapermen wryly commented in print, "We have put together this number under rather special conditions; in a shack that barely covers our heads, amid carpenters, gas workers, blacksmiths, and painters, dizzy from the unaccustomed air, dust, and noise and tired by the climb up . . . because the tower's elevators are not working yet."[31]

Despite the incomplete work on the elevators, Eiffel decided the time had come to celebrate the tower's completion. On April 1, 1889, he hosted the first of several celebratory gatherings. This included a huge party with champagne and a picnic for all the workers and their families, and another party for the engineers and designers. Eiffel also led a parade of government officials and members of the press to the top of the tower. Because the elevators were not yet functional, the group had to climb the stairs. The ascent to the first level alone took over an hour thanks to the frequent stops Eiffel made along the way to proudly point out various features of his masterpiece.

That afternoon Eiffel further celebrated his triumph by personally raising an enormous flag—a *tricolore*, the national flag of France—at the top of the tower. As the flag fluttered in the wind, a twenty-five-gun salute boomed from the first level to publicly proclaim the tower's completion. During the festivities one of Eiffel's engineers gave a stirring toast that sums up the tower's importance: "We salute the flag of 1789, which our fathers bore so proudly, which won so many victo-

The tower's narrow spiral staircases could only accommodate crowds walking up or down in single-file lines. As if to illustrate this fact, Gustave Eiffel (left) and a friend pose for a photograph on one of the tower's staircases.

ries, and which witnessed so much progress in science and humanity. We have tried to raise an adequate monument in honor of the great date of 1789, wherefore the tower's colossal proportions."[32]

Eiffel and his team had a right to be ecstatic: They had achieved something that had never been done before and that many people had regarded as impossible. Furthermore, Eiffel had done it in an astonishingly short time, under budget and with a few serious accidents. Speaking about himself in the third person in his autobiography, Eiffel writes, "This tower is Monsieur Eiffel's magnum opus, and is a symbol of strength and difficulties overcome."[33]

CHAPTER FOUR

Public Reaction

The tower's formal completion at the end of March 1889 was hailed as a major milestone. Although finishing touches were still being made, the fair organizers were delighted with the project. The centerpiece of the exposition, the iron tower, was in place, and to the organizers it represented the great promise for the future that they had anticipated. Their feelings were summed up by a comment from Jules Simon, France's minister of fine arts, which he wrote for the official guide to the Eiffel Tower. In it he states,

> This masterpiece of the builder's art comes at its appointed hour, on the threshold of the twentieth century, to symbolize the age of iron we are entering. From the second platform, and above all from the upper-most [level], a panorama unfolds such as has never been seen by human eyes. . . . Nature and history are unrolled side by side in their most powerful guise. It is on the plain, stretched out beneath your feet, that the past comes to an end. It is here that the future will be fulfilled.[34]

Voices Rise in Protest

Every day Parisians had for two years watched with anticipation the rise of the intriguing tower that now dominated the skyline of their city. Some shared Eiffel's enthusiasm for the project, but others saw it as an insult to the beauty of Paris's architecture—a useless, ugly waste of money. Both before and during construction, a sizable and vocal segment of the French population had objected to Eiffel's vision. Barry Bergdoll writes, "Even as the tower pushed toward the clouds, a chorus of opposing voices rose in protest, attacking it as a meaningless gesture, devoid of function and too reminiscent of an industrial smokestack."[35]

Parisians had mixed views of Eiffel's grand design. Some enthusiastically awaited its completion while others viewed it as an eyesore or, worse, a safety hazard. Rumors swirled of the possibility that the enormous tower could sink into the Seine River (pictured).

Some of the concerns were farfetched; for example, that the tower would sink into the waters of the Seine or would act as a giant magnet capable of drawing nails from surrounding buildings. Some people also worried that the tower could act as a lightning rod, with the potential to attract flashes of intense electricity and cause widespread fires. And others speculated that people would simply tire of the tower's novelty. In April 1888 a *New York Times* reporter commented, "The public may go up to its summit occasionally, but having once gazed [from it] said public will go where it can find things more interesting."[36]

Dire Prophecies

But some of the public's objections stemmed from real and legitimate concerns about safety. Even when it was still a proposal, countless people warned that Eiffel's design was unstable and predicted that the tower, if it were ever built, would surely collapse. These dire prophecies, which counted among their supporters many journalists and other public figures, inspired such newspaper headlines as "Eiffel Suicide!" and "Gustave Eiffel has gone mad."[37]

In addition to journalists and ordinary citizens, supposedly knowledgeable professionals also warned that the tower could collapse from its own weight. Bill Bryson notes, "A professor of mathematics filled reams of paper with calculations and concluded that when the tower was two-thirds up, the legs would splay and the whole would collapse in a thunderous fury, crushing the neighborhood below."[38]

Not surprisingly, fears about the tower's safety were especially strong among people who lived and worked adjacent to the Champ de Mars. The neighborhoods around the tower site consisted of low-rise houses, workshops, and small factories as well as large private houses and blocks of expensive apartments. Despite the significant social and economic differences of these various neighbor-hoods, the residents and businesses were united in their objections to the tower. Worries about their neighborhoods being turned into a massive construction site led to a number of legal actions against Eiffel. He was able to defuse these actions by promising to fully compensate the owners of the buildings for any damage his tower might cause.

"A Truly Tragic Street Lamp"

One further objection—that it was nothing more than an ugly eyesore—was perhaps as widely discussed among Parisians as any fears over safety. Especially concerned about this aspect of the tower were artists, writers, and others who were concerned with the aesthetics of their beloved and famously beautiful city. One critic, the novelist Léon Bloy, summarized this sentiment when he scornfully characterized the tower as "a truly tragic street lamp."[39]

Bloy was a member of the city's most prominent group of critics. This was the Committee of Three Hundred, so named to represent both the group's membership and the tower's height of three hundred meters. The group had formed before construction began and contin-ued its vocal objections long afterward. The group's leader was noted architect Charles Garnier. This was an ironic turn of events, since Garnier had been on the commission that reviewed the various tower proposals—and had joined the other members of the commission in approving Eiffel's design. Why Garnier later changed his mind is un-clear. In any case, Eiffel was happy to point out Garnier's about-face to reporters. He noted with glee that Garnier's inconsistency raised questions about his reliability as a judge of the rapidly progressing project.

The Committee of Three Hundred felt that building the tower at all was bad enough—but the group was especially concerned that it was slated to stay up for twenty years. To express their displeasure, the group wrote "A Protest Against the Eiffel Tower." Published as an open letter in the newspaper Le Temps in February 1887, the

A lightning bolt strikes the top of the Eiffel Tower during a violent thunderstorm. Early on some Parisians feared that the tower would act as a lightning rod and spark fires.

document melodramatically warned of the terrible influence the tower would have on some of Paris's most famous monuments:

> To bring our arguments home, imagine for a moment a giddy, ridiculous tower dominating Paris like a gigantic black smoke-stack, crushing under its barbaric bulk Notre Dame, the Tour Saint-Jacques, the Louvre, the Dome of les Invalides, the Arc de Triomphe, all our humiliated monuments will disappear in this ghastly dream. And for twenty years, we shall see stretching over the entire city, still trembling with the genius of so many centuries, like a blot of ink, the hateful shadow of the hateful column of bolted sheet metal.[40]

Brushing Off Criticisms

Despite such eloquent complaints, some of the tower's critics changed their minds after seeing the completed structure. They conceded that it had its own appeal, although its size may still have been daunting. A reporter for the (London) *Times* commented, "Even some of those who protested most loudly against the proposal now admit that the effect of the structure is not what they anticipated. They acknowledge that it has a light and graceful appearance, in spite of its gigantic size, and that it is an imposing monument, not unworthy of Paris."[41]

Despite such changes of heart, however, disdain of the tower on the part of some critics did not completely fade away. Eiffel brushed off all such criticisms and continued to vigorously defend his project. He never wavered in his belief that the tower would prove to be a monument to the marriage of science and art and a suitable symbol of the fair's themes. On the same day the Committee of Three Hundred published its declaration, an interview appeared in the same newspaper in which Eiffel compared his tower to the Great Pyramid of Egypt:

Because we are engineers, do people think that we do not care about the beauty of our constructions and that as well as making them strong and durable we do not to try to make them elegant? . . . Why should what is admirable in Egypt become hideous and ridiculous in Paris? I have thought about it and I admit I do not understand. . . .

When you want to see Notre Dame, you go and stand on the square in front of it. How could the tower, on the Champ de Mars, bother someone standing on the square in front of Notre Dame, where he cannot even see it? Besides, it is one of the most mistaken notions, although widely held, even by artists, that a tall edifice will crush the surrounding buildings.[42]

Finally Open to the Public

The barrage of criticism from some quarters notwithstanding, much of the public eagerly awaited the official opening of the tower on the day the grand fair also opened: May 6, 1889. Although the elevators were still balky and visitors were obliged to ascend and descend via the staircases for the first few days, public enthusiasm and curiosity remained high. In fact, the prospect of ascending to the top of the structure remained, for many, the most alluring aspect of the fair. Bergdoll comments, "The tower was one of the most-photographed buildings in Paris, if not the world, even before its much-marveled elevators first took visitors to the summit."[43]

WORDS IN CONTEXT

abyss
Bottomless pit.

Those who made the trek to the top, especially before the elevators began working, developed a greater appreciation for the tower's awe-inspiring height. Because the staircases were so narrow, traffic could only go one way. This meant that visitors could not change their

BEATING THE EIFFEL TOWER

Many nations were upset that the French had succeeded in creating the world's tallest structure. Comments were especially spiteful in the United States, where the Washington Monument, once the world's tallest structure, now ranked second behind the Eiffel Tower. Referring to the East River, which separates Manhattan from the rest of New York, *Harper's Weekly* magazine fumed, "Yes, fairly lofty; but lay it flat, and it would not span the East River. As to height, well, take an elevator in any building in New York, and if you want dizzy you can have quite enough of that kind of thing." American architects immediately began to draw up a variety of plans to best the French, including one in New York City that would feature a statue of an angel with a trumpet, announcing to the world the superiority of American industry and business sense.

There were also proposals to build a gigantic structure for the World's Columbian Exposition in Chicago (named for its honoree, Christopher Columbus) in 1893. Eiffel submitted a proposal, which was angrily rejected because he was not an American. Other ideas included creating a 9,000-foot tower (2,743 m) that would have cables strung from it capable of transporting people by "tobogganing" to and from New York, Boston, and other cities. Another idea involved a 4,000-foot tower (1,219 m) that would essentially be an elevator on the end of a giant bungee cord. The engineer who proposed it suggested that the area beneath the elevator have 8 feet (2.43 m) of featherbedding on it. These ideas were rejected in favor of another: the world's first Ferris wheel, which soared about 300 feet (91.4 m) over the fair.

Quoted in Jill Jonnes, *Eiffel's Tower.* New York: Viking, 2009, p. 136.

minds once they had begun the climb to the top. American writer Edyth Kirkwood admitted that, although she otherwise loved her visit, as she climbed the narrow stairs she thought unkind things about Eiffel for not making his stairs wide enough for people to change their minds.

In addition to the balky elevators, other problems occurred in the first days after the tower opened. For example, a workman knocked over a bucket of yellow paint, splattering a visitor. (The sightseer was later reimbursed for the cost of his clothes.) More seriously, a metal bolt crashed through the glass ceiling of the office of *Le Figaro*, piercing a seat that one of the newspaper's staff had just vacated. One writer for the newspaper commented that he wanted to remind Eiffel that the tower's public levels were meant to be public viewing platforms, not battlefields.

Despite these and other problems, a proud Eiffel was the first to sign the visitor guest book. On the first day he also hosted a party for family and friends at one of the restaurants on the first level. He spent the rest of that day watching all of the commotion taking place around and on the tower. Eiffel was understandably delighted to see the huge crowds that waited in line to experience ascending his tower, and by extension to take part in an event that was thrillingly new, huge, and modern.

A Thrilling Adventure

Even after the excitement of the opening days subsided, the tower proved to be a roaring success. Every day, long lines of tourists waited patiently to buy tickets. Prices varied, depending on which level a visitor wanted to get to, but they were generally affordable—and tickets were half-price on Sundays. The cheapest tickets were for those who chose to climb the stairs, not ride the elevators.

WORDS IN CONTEXT
panorama
Wide view.

In all, 2 million people ventured up the tower during the fair—from May 6 to October 31, 1889—and the lines did not abate even after the exposition closed. Eiffel's faith in his structure's popularity was clearly justified. A few weeks after the tower opened to the public, a number of newspapers around the world reported that Paris was ecstatic about the Eiffel Tower.

After waiting patiently in line for tickets, sightseers experienced a thrilling adventure, beginning with the elevator ride. Tak-

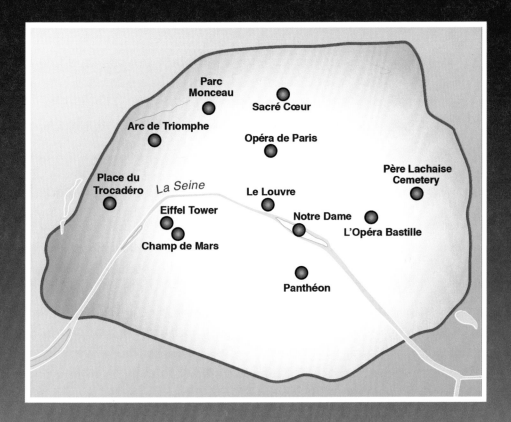

ing the elevator to the top floor put a visitor 187 feet (57 m) off the ground. Few people at the time had ever been this high up. The ride up proved to be remarkably smooth, and the public's enthusiasm for the elevators seemed to be barely affected by the fact that their mechanisms were deafeningly noisy. One reporter noted that visitors were "completely suspended over the abyss. However there is no feeling of danger. The great solid . . . machine ascends and descends majestically, without the slightest shock or inequality in its movements that could cause alarm, and the most timid of those who ascend to the second platform do so with a feeling of perfect security."[44]

Whether they rose in the elevators or climbed the stairs, visitors had astonishing views through the open girders, culminating in the expansive panorama at the top. Adding to the experience was the thrilling, stomach-clenching illusion that a person could fall from a dizzying height at any moment. Although perception of this danger was all too real for some people, Eiffel's long-standing concern for safety made the possibility of an accident highly unlikely. He had carefully installed such features as handrails, guardrails, and a series of nets to make sure visitors remained safe.

Gazing at Paris from Above

Those who braved the danger (real or imagined) were amply rewarded when they reached the tower's first level. The main attraction was the spectacular view from the observation deck that circled the tower; from this deck, all of Paris spread out at a visitor's feet. But many other attractions drew the attention of visitors as well. For example, visitors could buy treats from a pastry shop, or *patisserie*, have a drink at the bar, or hear a lecture or musical recital in the theater. Naturally, considering the tower's location in a city world famous for its love of food, they could also dine in one of several restaurants. The restaurants received mixed reviews, and the consensus was that the novelty of having a meal high in the air was the best thing about them. Those who did not formally dine at the tower could buy picnic provisions from vendors on the ground.

Overall, the public areas of the tower had a bustling, lively atmosphere. One visitor noted that visiting the tower was like visiting a city that was hanging in the rigging of an immense ship. Tourists could visit the offices and printing press of *Le Figaro*, the newspaper that was producing special "Eiffel Tower" editions. They could also visit kiosks on the first level to rent binoculars, buy tobacco or drinks, or purchase a wide array of guidebooks, photos, and other items.

Among the souvenirs available from these kiosks (as well as from vendors at the base of the tower and in nearby shops) were countless

AVOIDING THE TOWER AT ALL COSTS

According to legend, one member of the Committee of Three Hundred, the novelist Guy de Maupassant, often ate lunch in one of the tower's restaurants. He claimed that he did so because it was the only point in Paris from which he could not see the despised structure.

This story is probably only that: a story. For one thing, as Eiffel himself pointed out, the tower is not visible from most Paris streets. Furthermore, zoning restrictions limit the height of most buildings to seven stories, so only a very few of the taller buildings have a clear view of the tower. De Maupassant would have little cause for complaint on those grounds.

varieties of trinkets and mementos. They included drawings, sculptures, and paintings of the tower, as well as portraits of Eiffel himself. Visitors could also buy such items as tower-related handkerchiefs, caps, candlesticks, chocolate, cigar cases, jewelry, clocks, snuffboxes, umbrella handles, or sleeve buttons. Women could even buy chic dresses with ascending layers of collars—the perfect outfit, its creator said, to wear while visiting the tower.

Famous Guests

Members of the general public were by no means the only visitors to the tower. Many celebrities also made the journey to the top of the amazing new structure. One of these was the most famous inventor and engineer in the world: Thomas Edison. Edison had admired Eiffel's project from the very beginning. At an exhibit of drawings in Paris during the proposal stage of the tower, the renowned inventor had noted in a guest book, "To M. Eiffel, the Engineer, the brave builder of so gigantic and original a specimen of modern engineering from one who has the greatest admiration for all Engineers including the great Engineer *le bon Dieu* [the good God]."[45]

Edison was also a guest of honor when he visited the completed tower in mid-August 1889. After traveling to the top he pronounced both the structure and the view magnificent—a fitting monument to the technical skill and artistic vision of its creator. Comparing France to Great Britain, Edison (an American) stated, "The Tower is a great idea. The glory of Eiffel is in the magnitude of the conception and the nerve in the execution. I like the French. They have big conceptions. The English ought to take a leaf out of their books. What Englishman would have had this idea? What Englishman could have conceived the Statue of Liberty?"[46]

The great inventor was not the tower's only distinguished guest. The Prince of Wales, who would become England's King Edward VII, took in the sights. So did the emperor of Germany, the shah of Persia (now Iran), and a prince of Siam (now Thailand). In general, it seemed as though all of Parisian society was also smitten with the tower, and joining one's friends there became the fashionable thing to do. Using the French name for the structure, Tour Eiffel, Edyth Kirkwood commented, "High and low, rich and poor, are, for once, of one mind. Merriment, joy, feasting, succeed in a giddy whirl. . . . 'Meet me under the Tour Eiffel!' is the general cry for a rendezvous."[47]

Even Guy de Maupassant, the writer who had been one of the tower's most vocal critics, felt obliged to visit. He had no choice, de Maupassant complained, if he wanted to maintain a social life: "Friends no longer dine at home or accept a dinner invitation at your home. When invited, they accept only on condition that it is for a banquet on the Eiffel Tower—they think it gayer that way. As if obeying a general order, they invite you there every day of the week for either lunch or dinner."[48]

A Triumph

In almost every sense the structure was a success. The public loved it. It was a huge technological, artistic, and financial success. And fears about its safety proved groundless. The triumph was a particular victory for Eiffel, of course. He had remained true to his vision, organized an enormous team to make his vision a reality, and completed the project in record time. Despite facing seemingly impossible odds, Eiffel was enjoying a level of success that comes to few people.

The Exposition Universelle had proved to be a spectacular accomplishment. But the world's fair was also a relatively short-lived event, and its gates closed on October 31, 1889—less than six months after they had opened. To mark this occasion a fireworks display from atop the tower lit up the Parisian night sky. Eiffel had the good fortune to stage this last show against an appropriately dramatic background: a brilliantly clear night with a full moon. It was a good omen for a structure that was slated to come down in only twenty years.

CHAPTER FIVE

The Eiffel Tower Today

According to Eiffel's original contract with the city of Paris, his tower would stay up for only twenty years. After that, in 1909, the tower was scheduled to be dismantled, and the City of Paris would sell the metal as scrap. But that did not happen. Tourists continued to visit the Eiffel Tower long after the fair had closed, and within a year after the tower opened to the public its builder had recouped his construction costs. Already well-off, Eiffel was well on his way to becoming even wealthier. And fortunately for the tower's admirers, the plan to dismantle the structure was never carried out. The tower's usefulness as a radio transmitter, especially during World War I, ensured that it would continue to stay up. With millions of visitors every year, the Eiffel Tower today remains one of the most visited and admired structures in the world.

Visiting the Tower

Over the years the tower has not lost its appeal: An estimated 200 million people have visited the tower since it opened. Well over 7 million ascended it in 2011 alone. This makes the structure the most visited paid attraction in the world. It is also one of the most easily recognized landmarks in the world. A 2012 poll indicated that more British tourists recognized the Eiffel Tower than such iconic

The Eiffel Tower is one of the most recognized landmarks in the world. According to one recent poll, it is even more recognizable than the pyramids of Egypt or San Francisco's Golden Gate Bridge (pictured).

structures as the Sydney Opera House in Australia, San Francisco's Golden Gate Bridge, the pyramids of Egypt, or their own country's Stonehenge, Trafalgar Square, and the giant Ferris wheel called the London Eye.

The Eiffel Tower is open every day of the year. As was true in Eiffel's time, tourists can use the stairs or take the elevator and, as in the past, ticket prices are lower for those who use the stairs. Both the elevators and stairs lead to the first and second levels, but the elevator is the only way to access the third level, parts of which are open to the public.

Those who choose to make the trip on foot can judge the distance they have traveled by noting the regular signs that count off the number of steps. This number has varied slightly over the years, due to various renovations. Today, getting to the public areas on foot means climbing 1,665 steps, including the few steps that take visitors from the ground to the ticket booths at the base of the tower, as well as those leading from the third level landing to an upper observation platform. (The first and second levels are also both wheelchair accessible.) A popular option is to take the elevator up and climb down.

Whether ascending in the elevators or on foot, visitors can do much more than simply enjoy the thrilling panorama of Paris. A small museum and other displays on all of the viewing levels provide glimpses into the tower's history. Also, Eiffel's private apartment and lab on the top platform have been restored to their original condition, with wax figures standing in for Eiffel and Edison. Furthermore, visitors can mail letters directly from a post office in the tower, and between December and February up to eighty people at a time can even ice-skate on the first level—or simply watch the skaters while sipping hot chocolate, coffee, or wine. The rink is small but has proved to be very popular. In 2010 over one thousand people per day strapped on a pair of skates there. (Admission to the rink and skate rental are both included in the price of a ticket.) Something else that visitors can take advantage of is a special exhibit on the first level for children six to ten years old. It is designed to teach them about the history, construction, and importance of the tower.

Naturally, visitors can also eat and drink in the tower. Currently, it has two restaurants: *Le 58 Tour Eiffel*, a casual bar-restaurant on the first level, and *Le Jules Verne*, an expensive and elegant restaurant on the second floor with its own private elevator. Visitors also can buy informal snacks, such as sandwiches and soft drinks, or, to toast a special occasion, glasses of Champagne. Or they can bring their own food for a picnic.

⬡ A HUGE ELEVATOR

One of the major challenges for any tall construction project is the problem of lifting dozens of workers and huge amounts of building material up high. When Eiffel first built his tower, he solved the problem by using specially designed creeper elevators. These rose on tracks that went up the insides of each leg of the tower, going higher as each leg grew.

In 2012, the authorities responsible for maintaining the Eiffel Tower faced a similar problem as they planned for a major renovation project. Specifically, they wondered, what would be the best way to lift staff and materials to the first level of the structure? These materials were needed to complete extensive renovations of the restaurant and other public spaces.

One part of the solution was to build a gigantic transport platform—the construction industry's term for huge, custom-built, open elevators used for this purpose. A Finnish firm, Scanclimber, was hired to build the world's largest transport platform for the job. It weighs about 2 tons (1.8 metric tons) and can rise to about 200 feet (61 m) above the ground, just below the first floor. The area of the platform is about 79 x 21 feet (24 x 6 m), and it can carry up to 9.9 tons (9 metric tons) of material and people at a time. When the work is complete, the platform will be dismantled.

Maintaining the Tower

As they ascend and descend the tower, visitors can also see some of its inner workings at certain points. For example, the cable mechanism of the north leg's elevator can be viewed when exiting the elevator car. Often, visitors can also catch a glimpse of the machinery of the east and west elevators in action in their respective bases. However, this mechanism requires regular maintenance, and at these times the public is not admitted.

Not surprisingly, the Eiffel Tower requires constant maintenance for these and other parts of the structure. For this task the city of Paris, which still owns the tower, created a public utility, the

Société d'Exploitation de la Tour Eiffel (SETE). SETE oversees not just maintenance but also all of the other jobs that are needed to keep the structure open. SETE then gives the majority of the profits from the tower back to the city.

Today some five hundred employees handle the tower's operations. They work in its restaurants, keep the machinery in order and make repairs to the structure, operate its elevators, provide security, direct crowds headed in and out, and more. Some employees belong to specialized crews, such as the group charged with repainting the tower every seven years. Typically, a different color

 THE MAN WHO SOLD THE EIFFEL TOWER—TWICE!

The Eiffel Tower has been the object of numerous stunts and hoaxes over the years, but no crimes have been committed—except one. This was a deception executed in 1925 by a con man named Victor Lustig. Lustig's bold deception: He "sold" the Eiffel Tower.

Posing as an official of the city of Paris, he gathered a group of wealthy scrap metal merchants together and told them that the city was planning to dismantle the tower because it had become too expensive to maintain. He then offered to sell the iron to the highest bidder. The plan, he said, had to be kept secret to avoid public outcry.

One of these dealers, who was greatly in debt, agreed to pay Lustig, thinking that it would be a profitable investment. When Lustig later told the scrap dealer that he wanted an extra amount of money as a bribe, the dealer agreed. The dealer paid both amounts of money, and Lustig promptly left the country. He was never caught because the scrap dealer was too embarrassed to report the crime to the police. The story came out after Lustig returned to Paris when the money ran out. He tried to pull the scam again, but this time the victim reported Lustig to the police. The scam artist escaped arrest and fled to the United States, where he executed several more cons until he was captured in 1935 and sentenced to twenty years in prison, where he died in 1947.

is chosen each time the tower is repainted, with a public vote taken to determine this choice. (Visitors can vote using kiosks located near the tower's ticket booths.) Not all of the tower's surfaces receive exactly the same shade of paint, however, when a new coat is added. Different shades of a specific color are used, with the lightest at the top. This creates the illusion for people on the ground that the tower is taller.

Another specialized crew is responsible for replacing, as needed, the approximately twenty thousand lightbulbs used to illuminate the tower at night. This array of bulbs produces a sparkling display every night, outlining the tower's shape once every hour from dusk until 1:00 a.m. Some three hundred spotlights arrayed around the tower also dramatically light up the structure at night, and beacons atop the tower, visible from up to 50 miles (80.5 km) away, sweep the area. On occasion, extra lighting is installed to create light shows and fireworks displays for special events.

How the Tower Has Changed

Over the years the tower has undergone a variety of small modifications from its original state, as well as major renovations. One example of a small change concerns the seventy-two names that were originally engraved on the sides of the tower, just under the first level. Each of these names was about 24 inches (60 cm) high. Eiffel had them placed there to honor seventy-two scientists and engineers—some of whom date back to the era of the French Revolution—because their experiments and discoveries had significantly contributed to the monument's construction. The names of these scientists were covered over early in the twentieth century, but during a major renovation in 1986–1987 they were restored to their original state and painted in gold, as they had been when the tower was built.

Parisians enjoy an evening of ice skating almost 230 feet above street level on a small rink located on the first level of the Eiffel Tower. Other attractions, besides the tower itself, include a museum and restaurants.

Other changes made over the years have included restoring the original facades of the first floor, which had been covered over early in the twentieth century. The method of lighting up the tower has also been improved. In particular, gas lamps that originally lit its outline at night have now been replaced by some twenty thousand electric lightbulbs.

More substantial changes include updates of the elevator systems. For example, in 1965 a sharply increasing number of visitors prompted the use of new procedures and equipment for the elevators in all four legs. In the years since, the systems have been further upgraded with computer-controlled procedures. (The original elevators had been run by operators who sat in precarious cages below the machines. Today, visitors can see the position of one of these operators, replaced by a mannequin.)

The original elevators were gradually scrapped, the last of them in 1982 after nearly a century of service. Today, all of the cars in use are relatively standard. The current elevators are capable of carrying more than one hundred people per trip and making a dozen round trips every hour. Workers have also installed emergency staircases, adding to the originals. Other modifications include the use of petroleum products to grease the elevators' mechanisms, replacing the original material: ox or pig fat mixed with hemp.

Renovating the Tower

In addition to the various other changes that the tower has undergone over the years, a major renovation project was scheduled for 2012–2013, at an estimated cost of 25 million euros (about $32

US million). The entire cost was covered by SETE. The work was scheduled to last eighteen months (during which time the tower was to remain open). This project marked the first major renovation of the tower since 1986–1987. "We're hoping to give ourselves the tools we need to move into the next century,"[49] Jean-Bernard Bros, president of SETE, stated in October 2012.

In large part the renovations were needed because of the sharp increase in the number of visitors. According to SETE, in 2011, more people ascended the tower since the renovation of 1986–1987 than did so in the entire first century of its existence. By 2011, it was increasingly clear that the tower's public spaces were too cramped and inefficiently organized to accommodate these ever-increasing crowds.

The planned restoration included major makeovers of the first level. For example, SETE planned to rebuild the reception and conference rooms to make them more attractive as event spaces. Plans also called for updating restrooms, shops, restaurants, and other visitor services to make them more attractive, better able to accommodate large crowds, and easier to maintain. Possibly the biggest change was the addition of a huge glass floor in part of the first level's public space to allow visitors to see the city directly below. This glass floor was to cover about 5,500 square feet (511 sq m).

Smaller renovations included a new look for the restaurants and improved shelters from the weather for those who are waiting for elevators. And SETE planned to create new exhibits for the museum, improve the educational film program, and expand other features of the tower's displays. Still another planned addition included a giant mural of two hundred unpublished historical photos of the tower, for display on the ground floor near the ticket booths.

In addition to updating the look and operation of the tower, the renovation project was to add a number of environmentally friendly new features. These included improved energy efficiency by converting to solar and wind energy for partially heating and lighting the tower. Other improvements were to make the tower more readily accessible to people with disabilities.

The Tower Remains Standing

Renovations and everything else about the tower could not have happened if the original plan to scrap the tower had come to pass. There were several reasons why this plan was abandoned. One arose simply out of sentimentality and affection. As the end of the contract between Eiffel and Parisian authorities drew near, huge numbers of people had come to love the tower and understand its importance. A massive protest would surely have erupted if the original plan had been carried out. And so in 1906 the city officially approved five more years of life for the tower, a condition that was in time made permanent.

Not everyone was enthusiastic about the decision to keep the tower. Among the critics were some Parisian government authorities who considered the structure, if nothing else, simply too expensive to maintain. They were at best lukewarm at the prospect of keeping the tower and indicated that they would have preferred that it had not been built in the first place. Overall, the attitude among these

 EIFFEL TOWERS AROUND THE WORLD

In the decades since it was built, a number of smaller replicas or variations of Eiffel's masterpiece have appeared around the world. These include the 518-foot Blackpool Tower (158 m) in Blackpool, England, which was finished in 1894 and was directly inspired by the Eiffel Tower. There is also a 70-foot wooden replica (21.3 m) in the small town of Paris, Tennessee; and a half-size tower that is part of a casino and hotel complex, Paris Las Vegas, in Las Vegas, Nevada. And yet another tower is in a Texas town, also named Paris: This tower is a 65-foot version (19.8 m), topped off by a 10-foot-wide cowboy hat (3 m).

authorities was one of tired acceptance. As one Parisian official commented, "If [the Eiffel Tower] did not exist, one would probably not contemplate building it there, or even perhaps anywhere else; but it does exist."[50]

Eiffel's Scientific Research

Beyond the sentimental feelings of the public, Eiffel had a more practical reason for keeping the tower. Part of his private quarters on the third level was devoted to a small laboratory. In the decades after the fair Eiffel conducted numerous experiments there, including the study of the effects of air resistance and atmospheric pressure on structures such as his.

Eiffel's experiments also proved something that he had championed all along: the use of the tower as a superb radio transmitter. Eiffel had first demonstrated this ability in 1898, when he and a fellow scientist, Eugene Ducretet, successfully sent a radio message from Eiffel's lab to a location about 2.5 miles (4 km) away. Today this feat seems primitive, but at the time radio was a revolutionary and largely untested new technology. Eiffel's accomplishment was a landmark event.

WORDS IN CONTEXT

euro
The unit of money used by the nations of the European Union.

Eiffel's success in sending radio signals proved to be crucial to the future of the tower. He demonstrated that the structure could be a practical tool for communication. This aspect of the tower's usefulness was proven during the First World War (1914–1918), when French military authorities used it to jam the signals of their enemy, Germany. This achievement was a significant factor in the German army's failure to capture Paris, which in turn helped France and its allies win the war.

After that, radio transmissions from the tower became commonplace. Radio France, the national system, began regular broadcasts from it in 1922, followed soon by primitive television signals. In 1957 and again in 1981, the installation of improved radio/television antennas raised the tower's overall height to its current height of 1,069 feet (325 m). The antennas on the tower today carry broadcasts for six TV networks and dozens of radio stations.

More Danger

The prospect of dismantling the tower after twenty years was not the only threat it has faced. The structure was nearly destroyed during World War II (1939–1945). In 1940 the German Nazi army invaded and occupied Paris. The leader of the Nazis, Adolf Hitler, recognized that the tower was a powerful symbol of France's independence. He ordered it torn down, in part as a way to demoralize the nation and to assert his control over Paris.

According to a 1941 article in the Australian newspaper *Argus*, Hitler had other reasons to dismantle the tower. He wanted to demolish the structure because it had no artistic or historic value. His idea was to use the iron as scrap material for the German war effort, which was in great need of the metal to build weapons.

Obviously, this never happened. The exact reason is not clear. One likely explanation is that the Germans lacked the equipment they needed to dismantle the tower. However, there are also indications that the Nazi military governor in Paris never carried out Hitler's orders because he did not want to be known afterward as the man who destroyed the Eiffel Tower. In any case, the structure became a symbolic battleground.

Hitler was photographed in front of it as a show of power, but otherwise the Germans were largely thwarted in their plans. French resistance fighters cut the cables for the elevators, so that the Nazis would be hampered in reaching the top. German soldiers were able to climb it, however, and they briefly exchanged the French flag with one displaying the swastika symbol of the Nazis. (The German flag was so big that it blew away in the wind and was not replaced.) When Paris was liberated near the end of the war, the French flag once again flew proudly from the top of the tower.

The Eiffel Tower at night is a sight to behold. Recent renovation plans included the use of solar and wind energy for some of the tower's heat and lighting. Additional plans called for a makeover of the first level, including the addition of a huge glass floor that will allow visitors to see the city directly below.

In the 1960s the Eiffel Tower again faced a threat. At that time secret negotiations between the French and Canadian governments were taking place. (These talks were not revealed to the public until the 1980s.) The idea was to temporarily move the Eiffel Tower to Montreal, the main city in the Canadian province of Quebec, as part of that city's world's fair, Expo 67. Reportedly, the plan was canceled because the company that operated the tower was afraid that it might not be possible to reassemble the tower in its original location.

Suicides and Stunts

The Nazis and others who have threatened the tower over the years are not the only unhappy aspects of the Eiffel Tower's existence. One facet of its public nature is the number of people who commit suicide by jumping from it. Despite extensive safety measures, an estimated four hundred people have killed themselves there. The French police and the operators of the tower decline to give out exact numbers, stating only that the number of deaths is too high. A spokesman for the organization that operates the tower comments, "Some years it's two or three, some years none at all. We don't talk about it because we don't want to give people ideas."[51] At the same time, tall structures are often irresistible to daredevils who love to perform risky or crazy stunts, and over the years the Eiffel Tower has not escaped this. The first (and one of the most unusual) of these stunts was performed in 1889, while the fair was still in progress, by a man who climbed to the second level on stilts. He was from the rural region of Les Lands, where shepherds used stilts to walk around marshy ground without getting wet and to keep an eye on their flocks from a distance. A writer for the newspaper office in the tower noted that the intrepid stilt-walker walked around the public areas, to the great astonishment of everyone present.

More recently, other risk-takers and attention-seekers have performed a variety of other highly public stunts. Mountaineers have climbed it. Skateboarders, rollerbladers, and bicyclists have ridden down its stairs, or off ramps beginning at its lower level. Parachutists and bungee jumpers have launched themselves from it, and trapeze artists have performed high atop it. In 1989, to commemorate the one hundredth anniversary of the tower, the famous French tightrope walker Philippe Petit walked a wire that had been strung between the Place du Trocadéro (Trocadéro Square) and the second level of the tower, a distance of some 2,300 feet (700 m). Petit's achievement and most of the other stunts performed over the years have been successful. Unfortunately, some have not. For example, a Norwegian parachutist who specialized in jumping from low heights died in 2005 after leaping from the second level and snagging his chute on the way down.

The tower has also been the target of several hoaxes. For example, in 2008 a number of media outlets, including such prestigious newspapers as England's *Guardian* and America's *New York Times*, fell for a hoax. The news outlets received a press release from the Parisian architectural firm Serero Architects. Though the firm is real, the press release was a phony. It claimed that Serero had won a bid to add a number of temporary additions to the tower. Notable among these was a modification of the top observation deck that would more than double its size, in honor of the structure's 120th birthday. The press release states in part,

> Serero analyzed how the monument's 6 million to 7 million annual visitors wish to explore the tower and found that roughly 95 percent want to go directly to the third floor. . . .

However, the small capacity of the existing . . . platform results in wait times of at least 35 minutes and as long as an hour and 10 minutes. . . .

To improve this situation, the firm has proposed a temporary third-level platform expansion that more than doubles the visitors' area. . . . Constructed of a lightweight carbon Kevlar material, steel connectors, and metal mesh in three separate structural components, the expanded deck would allow an estimated 1,700 visitors per hour to access the tower's top floor.[52]

Relying on this press release, the media reported on the planned renovations—only to discover soon after that it was a hoax perpetrated as a joke by the architectural firm.

"Eiffel *Is* the Tower"

Eiffel created his masterpiece to be more than just an object of stunts and hoaxes. His great tower remains far and away his best known creation, but in the years before and after that project he was key to a number of other challenging building projects. One of these—his involvement in the building of the Panama Canal—ended disastrously, when he was caught up in a scandal that resulted in bankruptcy for the project's organizer.

Eiffel continued to be active in other ways as well, including extensive experimentation in meteorology and telecommunications. He published thirty-one books and treatises. He swam and fenced well into his eighties, and he continued to garner honors and awards from governments around the world, including many monuments, streets, and other public locations named for him.

Nonetheless, to this day Eiffel remains intimately connected in the public eye with his tower. Summing up the public's attitude, Henri Loyrette comments, "Eiffel *is* the tower."[53] The engineer himself once said, only half-jokingly, "I ought to be jealous of the tower. It is much more famous than I am. People seem to think it is my only work, whereas I have done other things after all."[54]

Eiffel died on December 27, 1923, at the age of ninety-one. But he lives on in the form of the structure that bears his name—one of the great structures of the world.

SOURCE NOTES

Introduction: The Iron Lady

1. Quoted in Barry Bergdoll, introduction to *The Eiffel Tower: A Photographic Survey*, by Lucien Hervé. New York: Princeton University Press, 2003, p. 13.
2. Jill Jonnes, *Eiffel's Tower*. New York: Viking, 2009, p. 21.
3. Henri Loyrette, *Gustave Eiffel*. New York: Rizzoli, 1985, p. 148.
4. Bill Bryson, *At Home*. New York: Anchor, 2010, p. 254.
5. Quoted in Jonnes, *Eiffel's Tower*, p. 16.
6. Jonnes, *Eiffel's Tower*, p. 311.

Chapter One: The Background

7. Ly Y. Bui, "Plan of Champ de Mars, Paris 1889," A Treasury of World's Fair Art & Architecture, University of Maryland Libraries. http://hdl.handle.net/1903.1/308.
8. Quoted in Bui, "Plan of Champ de Mars, Paris 1889."
9. Quoted in John H. Lienhard, "Galerie des Machines," in *Engines of Our Ingenuity*, University of Houston College of Engineering. www.uh.edu.
10. Bill Bryson, *At Home*, p. 251.
11. Bertrand Lemoine, "Gustave Eiffel," in *The Great Builders*, Kenneth Powell, ed. London: Thames and Hudson, 2011, p. 142.
12. Henri Loyrette, *Gustave Eiffel*, p. 100.
13. Bill Bryson, *At Home*, p. 252.

Chapter Two: The Design

14. Quoted in Jill Jonnes, *Eiffel's Tower*, p. 25.
15. Barry Bergdoll, introduction to *The Eiffel Tower*, by Hervé, p. 10.
16. Henri Loyrette, *Gustave Eiffel*, p. 111.
17. Bill Bryson, *At Home*, p. 250.
18. Quoted in *Artdaily*, "Eiffel Tower, Symbol of France, Celebrates Its 120th Anniversary with Makeover," August 11, 2012. www.artdaily.org.

19. Bertrand Lemoine, "Gustave Eiffel," in *The Great Builders*, p. 141.

20. Quoted in Loyrette, *Gustave Eiffel*, p. 111.

21. Quoted in Loyrette, *Gustave Eiffel*, p. 206.

22. Quoted in *Arras France Tourism Guide*, "The Eiffel Tower in Paris." http://arras-france.com.

23. Annette Fierro, *The Glass State: The Technology of the Spectacle, Paris, 1981–1998*. Cambridge, MA: MIT Press, 2002, p. 51.

24. Quoted in *Artdaily*, "Eiffel Tower, Symbol of France."

25. Jonnes, *Eiffel's Tower*, p. 52.

Chapter Three: The Construction

26. Annette Fierro, *The Glass State*, p. 53.

27. Quoted in Caroline Sutton, *How Did They Do That?* New York: HarperCollins, 1985. http://books.google.com.

28. Henri Loyrette, *Gustave Eiffel*, p. 148.

29. Quoted in Jonnes, *Eiffel's Tower*, p. 41.

30. Quoted in Architect Leadership Council, "The Eiffel Tower." http://greenalc.com.

31. Quoted in Joseph Harriss, *The Tallest Tower*. Nashville, IN: Unlimited Publishing, 2008, p. 92.

32. Quoted in Jonnes, *Eiffel's Tower*, p. 90.

33. Quoted in Loyrette, *Gustave Eiffel*, p. 105.

Chapter Four: Public Reaction

34. Quoted in Barry Bergdoll, introduction to *The Eiffel Tower*, by Hervé, p. 9.

35. Bergdoll, introduction to *The Eiffel Tower*, by Hervé, p. 9.

36. Quoted in *New York Times*, "Next Year's Big Show," April 22, 1888. http://query.nytimes.com.

37. Quoted in *USAEurotravel*, "Eiffel Tower, Paris, France," June 7, 2012. http://europlaces.wordpress.com.

38. Bill Bryson, *At Home*, pp. 254–55.

39. Quoted in *Oxford Art Online*, "Rise of the Modern City." www.oxfordartonline.com.

40. Quoted in *Airship Paris*, "Eiffel Tower." www.airship-paris.fr/en/eiffel-tower.html.

41. Quoted in Jonnes, *Eiffel's Tower*, pp. 80–81.
42. Quoted in Jöelle Bolloch, "The Eiffel Tower," Faculty of Exact Sciences, Engineering, and Surveying, National University of Rosario, Argentina. www.fceia.unr.edu.ar.
43. Bergdoll, introduction to *The Eiffel Tower*, by Hervé, p. 8.
44. Quoted in Jonnes, *Eiffel's Tower*, p. 135.
45. Quoted in Bergdoll, introduction to *The Eiffel Tower*, by Hervé, p. 12.
46. Quoted in Neil Baldwin, *Edison: Inventing the Century*. Chicago: University of Chicago Press, 2001, p. 205.
47. Quoted in Jonnes, *Eiffel's Tower*, p. 201.
48. Quoted in Jonnes, *Eiffel's Tower*, p. 164.

Chapter Five: The Eiffel Tower Today

49. Quoted in *Telegraph* (UK), "Eiffel Tower Goes Green," October 22, 2012. www.telegraph.co.uk.
50. Quoted in Jonnes, *Eiffel's Tower*, p. 301.
51. Quoted in Jon Henley, "Eiffel Tower Stunt Kills Parachutist." *Guardian* (UK), May 17, 2005. www.guardian.co.uk/world/2005/may/18/france.jonhenley.
52. Quoted in Stephani Miller, "Eiffel Tower Redesign a Hoax," *Architect*, March 17, 2008. www.architectmagazine.com/design/eiffel-tower-redesign-a-hoax.aspx.
53. Henri Loyrette, *Gustave Eiffel*, p. 9.
54. Quoted in Jonnes, *Eiffel's Tower*, p. 308.

FACTS ABOUT THE EIFFEL TOWER

Measurements
- Base: 107,584 square feet (9,994.8 sq. m).
- Height of first platform: 187 feet (57 m).
- Height of second platform: 377.2 feet (115 m).
- Height of third platform: 905.5 feet (276 m).
- Height of the tower when built (including flagpole): 1,023.6 feet (312 m).
- Current height (including antennas): 1,069 feet (325 m).
- Height variation due to outside temperature: 6 inches (15 cm).
- Total weight: 11,023 tons (10,000 metric tons).
- The elevators travel approximately 62,137 miles (100,000 km) per year.
- Speed of the elevators: 6.56 feet (2 m) per second.
- Weight of iron: About 8,470 tons (7,300 metric tons). Total weight including nonmetal components: about 11,000 tons (10,000 metric tons).
- Total area of safety nets: 11,960 square yards (10,000 square m).

Construction
- A staff of fifty engineers and designers took two years to produce 1,700 general drawings and 3,629 detailed drawings.
- Seven million holes were drilled to make the tower. If laid end to end they would form a tube 43 miles (69 km) long.
- Construction required 18,038 pieces of iron and 2.5 million rivets.

Features
- Steps: A total of 1,665, but 669 to the second level (the highest accessible to public on foot).

- Twenty thousand lightbulbs light the monument at night for five minutes every hour on the hour.

Upkeep
- Painting: Requires 60 tons of paint, 25 painters, 1,500 brushes, and 15 months, done once every 7 years.

Visitors
- The tower received its 250 millionth visitor in 2010.
- About 75 percent of the 7.5 million visitors in 2011 were from other countries.

FOR FURTHER RESEARCH

Books

Sandra Forty, *Wonders of the World*. Charlottesville, VA: Taj Books, 2009.

Lucien Hervé, *The Eiffel Tower: A Photographic Survey*. New York: Princeton Architectural Press, 2003.

Ann Kerns, *Seven Wonders of Architecture*. Minneapolis: Twenty-First Century, 2010.

Nate Leboutillier, *Eiffel Tower*. Mankato, MN: Creative Education, 2009.

Ron Miller, *Seven Wonders of Engineering*. Minneapolis: Twenty-First Century, 2010.

Bryan Pezzi and Heather Kissock, *Eiffel Tower*. New York: Weigl, 2011.

Websites

The Construction of the Eiffel Tower (http://abcnews.go.com/Inter national/slideshow/eiffel-towers-construction-start-fin-ish-16041965). A site with interesting photos of the tower's design plans and construction phase, maintained by ABC News.

Eiffel Tower (www.eiffel-tower.com). The official website of the organization that manages the tower, with such information as history, statistics, and how to visit.

Gustave Eiffel (www.biography.com/people/gustave-eiffel-9285294). This site has a brief biography of the engineer.

Looking Up to the Eiffel Tower (www.time.com/time/photogallery /0,29307,1878708_1842694,00.html). This site from Time.com has some unusual photos from the tower's early days, including shots of the world's fair and of Eiffel in his lab.

Stunt on the Eiffel Tower (www.youtube.com/watch?v=vVqQpre WYh4). An amazing short video of acrobats performing near the top of the tower.

INDEX

Note: Boldface page numbers indicate illustrations.

abyss, defined, 58
aesthetics, defined, 54
Argus (Australian newspaper), 77
aristocrats, 13

Barcelona Exposition (1888), 27–28
Bartholdi, Frédéric, 24, 25
Bergdoll, Barry
   on design, 27
   on opposition to Tower, 53
   on popularity of Tower, 58
Blackpool Tower, 75
Bloy, Léon, 55
Bros, Jean-Bernard, 74
Bryson, Bill
   on choice of iron, 31
   on design, 11
   on Eiffel's early works, 22
   on Eiffel's motivation, 22
   example of prophecy of doom, 54
   on importance of skeleton, 25
   on Statue of Liberty, 36
budget, 26, 51
Bui, Ly Y., 16
Burj Khalifa, height of, 11, 12

caissons, 47
canteen, defined, 49
Carnot, Nicolas Sadi, 17–18
Champ de Mars, 16, 54
Chrysler Building, height of, 9, 12
Cody, Buffalo Bill, 18–19
Committee of Three Hundred, 55, 57, 63

Communards, 14
Compagnie des établissements Eiffel, 24–25
concept, 19
construction
   accuracy challenges, 33
   completion celebration, 49–51
   of elevators, 49
   of foundations, 40, 41
   groundbreaking ceremony, 40
   of iron pieces, 39
   number of factory laborers, 39
   number of on-site laborers, 41
   process, 41–44
   responsibility for surrounding area, 42
   safety and, 46, 47
   stages, 29, 45, 48–49
   time frame, 39
   underwater, 47
   use of prefabricated kits, 24
costs, 42
counterbalance, defined, 37
cranes, 43
creepers, defined, 43

De Maupassant, Guy, 63, 64
demolition
   Eiffel's opposition to, 76
   first delay of, 75
   Hitler and, 77
   Lustig scam and, 70
   original plans for, 66, 75
   use as radio transmitter, 66, 76–77
design
   absence of facade, 23

accuracy challenges, 33

agreement with Paris city officials, 26

bridge-building principles in, 27

competition entries, 19–21

contributions of Koechlin and Nougier, 27–29

contributions of Sauvestre, 30

drawings, 38

Eiffel and, 9, 11

elevators, 36–38

patents, 31–32

similarity to Exposición Universal (Universal Exposition) of 1888, 27

structural elements as decorative features, 23

time spent on, 38

weather/wind challenges, 34–36, 35

dimensions

height, 9, 11–12, **12**

of viewing platforms, 28

Ducretet, Eugene, 76

École Centrale des Arts et Manufactures, 21

Edison, Thomas, 19, 63–64

Edoux, Léon, 37–38

Eiffel, (Alexandre-)Gustave, **20**, **50**

characteristics of, 32, 39, 46

death of, 82

education of, 21

family of, 21

on Garnier, 55

Panama Canal and, 81

projects prior to Tower by, 22–25, 36

promises made by, 26, 32

proposal of, 21

reputation of, 9

role of, 9, 11

Tower and

apartment for, 28

on battle against wind, 34

on criticism of, 57–58

on fame of, 82

importance of, 8–9

on importance of, 51

motivation for, 22

opening day celebration of, 60

on painting, 36

workers and, 46, 47

World's Columbian Exposition proposal by, 59

Eiffel et Cie (Eiffel and Company), 23–24

Eiffel Tower, **10**, **15**, **53**, **56**, **73**, **78**

elevators

access to third level and, 67

companies hired to build, 49

for construction, 43

design of, 36–38

opening day difficulties, 58

since Exposition, 67–68, 72

ticket price and, 60, 67

for 2012 renovation, 69

visitors enthusiasm for, 61

Empire State Building, height of, 11, **12**

entrepreneur, defined, 9

environmental improvements, 74–75

euro, defined, 76

Evening Telegraph (British newspaper), 44

Expo 67, 79

Exposición Universal (Universal Exposition) of 1888, 27

Exposition Universelle de 1878, 23

Exposition Universelle de 1889, 15

after modifications, 71–72

operation and maintenance,
69–71
uses, 66
visitors, 66–68, 74
background of, 13–14, 17
closing day, 65
goals of, 14–16, 17
location, 16
motto, 16
opening day, 17, 58–60
pavilions and theme, 16–19
success of, 18
Tower and theme, 8, 19–20

facade, 23, 72
Ferris wheel, 59
Ferry, Jules, 14–16
Fierro, Annette, 34, 39
Figaro, Le (French newspaper), 21, 49, 60, 62
fireworks, 48, 65, 71
foundations, 40, 41
France, political and economic conditions, 14–15, 17
Franco-Prussian War (1870–1871), 14, 18
French Revolution, 13–14
fretwork, defined, 11

Galerie des Machines (Machinery Hall), 19
Garabit Viaduct, 24, 27
Garnier, Charles, 55
gas lamp, defined, 71
Gateway Arch, height of, 12
girder, defined, 28
Golden Gate Bridge, 67
Goudeau, Emile, 48
Great Pyramid of Egypt, comparison to, 57–58
Guardian (English newspaper), 80

Harper's Weekly (magazine), 59

height, 9, 11–12, **12**
hemp, defined, 72
Hitler, Adolf, 77
hoaxes, 70, 80–81
hydraulic jacks, defined, 46

ice skating, 68, 73
Imperial Diamond, 18
Industrial Revolution, 16
iron, 30
Iron Lady, 8

Jonnes, Jill
on elevators, 36–37
on Tower as artistic triumph, 8–9, 12

Kirkwood, Edyth, 59, 64
Koechlin, Maurice
design by, 27–29
Eiffel's promises to, 32
patent share, 31–32

Las Vegas Eiffel, 75
Le Corbusier, 8
legs
construction of, 29, 42, 43
in design, 21, 28
elevators and, 36, 37
foundations for, 40
Lemoine, Bertrand, 24, 32
Levallois-Perret factory, 39
lighting, 71, 72, 73, 78
lightning, 54, 56
Lockroy, Édouard, 11
Louis XVI (king of France), 13
Loyrette, Henri
on construction material, 31
on construction process, 42–43
on Koechlin and Nougier, 28
on role of Eiffel, 9, 11, 81
on Statue of Liberty, 24
Lustig, Victor, 70

Lycée Royale, 21

Machinery Hall, 19
maintenance, 69–71
Maria Pia bridge, 23
Marie Antoinette (queen of
    France), 13
masonry, 31
materials, choice of, 30–31

names on Tower, 71
New York Times (newspaper), 54,
    80
nickname, 8
Nougier, Émile
    design by, 27–29
    Eiffel's promises to, 32
    patent share, 31–32

Oakley, Annie, 19
Otis Elevator, 49

Panama Canal, 81
panorama, defined, 60
Paris Commune, 14
Paris landmarks, **61**
Paris, Tennessee, tower, 75
Paris, Texas, tower, 75
patisserie, defined, 64
Pest (Hungary) railway terminal, 23
Petit, Philippe, 80
Place du Trocadéro, 80
prefabricated, defined, 24
Prince of Wales (King Edward VII
    of England), 64
"Protest Against the Eiffel
    Tower, A" (Committee of Three
    Hundred), 55, 57
Prussia, 14
public reaction, 11–12
    international, 59
    objections, 52–53, 55, **56**, 57–58
    popularity

after 1889 Exposition, 8, 66–67,
    74
    during 1889 Exposition, 58–62
    praise, 52
    safety concerns, 54–55
publicity, 32–33
puddle iron, 30
purpose, 8, 19
pylons, 21, 27, 28, 31–32

Radio France, 76–77
radio transmission, 66, 76–77
rain challenges, 35–36
Reconciliation, Rehabilitation, and
    Imperial Supremacy, 16
renovation (2012–2013), 69, 72,
    74–75
repainting process, 35–36
replicas, 75
rivet, defined, 33
Roux, Combaluzier and Lepape, 49

safety
    features for visitors, 62
    measures during construction, 47
    Sauvestre and, 30
    suicide attempts, 79
sale of Tower, 70
Sauvestre, Stephen, 30, 32
scaffold innovations, 43
scaffolds, defined, 44
Scanclimber, 69
science and technology
    exhibits about, 19
    as Exposition theme, 16
    research by Eiffel, 76
Sears Tower, height of, 12
Serero Architects hoax, 80–81
Seyrig, Théophile, 23
Simon, Jules, 52
snow challenges, 35–36
*Société d'Exploitation de la Tour
    Eiffel* (SETE), 69–70, 74

souvenirs, 62–63
staircases, 50
    access to third level and, 67
    emergency, 72
    number of steps, 68
    stunts on, 80
    ticket price and, 60, 67
    use by public before elevators,
        58–59
Statue of Liberty, 24–25, 36
steel, 30–31
stonework, 31
stunts, 79–80
suicide attempts, 79
symbolism, 8, 33

television transmission, 76–77
temperature challenges, 34–35, 40
Temps, Le (French newspaper), 34,
    55, 57
Third Republic
    Exposition goal and, 16
    overview of, 17
    stability of, 14
Times (British newspaper), 57
Trocadéro Square, 80
truss, defined, 30

United States, reaction in, 59

visitors
    after 1889 Exposition, 66–68,
        74
    enthusiasm for elevators, 61
    famous, 63–64
    number during Exposition, 60
    opening day difficulties, 58–60
    restaurants, shops, attractions for,
        62–63, 68, 73, 74
    safety features for, 62

Washington Monument, height of,
    9, 12, 48, 59
weather
    challenges
        design, 34–36, 35
        gravel bed foundation and, 40
    fears of lightning, 54, 56
Wild West Show, 18–19
Wilhelm I (emperor of Prussia),
    14
wind resistance, 34–36, 35
workers
    conditions of, 44, 46, 47
    current, 70–71
working conditions, 44, 46, 47
World War I (1914–1918), 66, 76
World War II (1939–1945), 77
World's Columbian Exposition, 59

PICTURE CREDITS

ABOUT THE AUTHOR

Adam Woog has written many books for children, teenagers, and adults. He also teaches at a preschool. Woog and his wife, who have a grown daughter, live in Seattle, Washington.